THE SOCIETY OF THE LIVING DEAD

The Illustrated History of Ottawa's Radium Dial Scandal

Jim Ridings

Radium victims suing for compensation have formed The Society of the Living Dead, with the object of seeking better protection for victims of occupational diseases. From left are shown Thomas Donohue, husband of Catherine Donohue, a victim; L. J. Grossman, attorney for the group; Mrs. Charlotte Purcell, Mrs. Pearl Payne and Mrs. Marie Rossiter.

Copyright, 1938, by The Chicago Herald and Examiner. All rights reserved

America Through Time is an imprint of Fonthill Media LLC
www.through-time.com
office@through-time.com

Published by Arcadia Publishing by arrangement with Fonthill Media LLC
For all general information, please contact Arcadia Publishing:
Telephone: 843-853-2070
Fax: 843-853-0044
E-mail: sales@arcadiapublishing.com
For customer service and orders:
Toll-Free 1-888-313-2665

www.arcadiapublishing.com

First published 2020

Copyright © Jim Ridings 2020

ISBN 978-1-63499-229-9

Typeset in Mrs Eaves XL Serif Narrow
Printed and bound in England

CONTENTS

ACKNOWLEDGMENTS

A number of sources—from medical journals, newspapers, internet sources, and personal interviews—were used. Newspaper clippings are used as illustrations to best show how it really was at the time.

Special thanks to Linda Willibey; Katie (Dumke) Troccoli; Darlene Halm; Patty Gray; Jeff Ratajczak, executive director, LaSalle County Historical Society Museum; Ken Ricci; Ed Carroll; Gloria Boone; Mike and Laurie Pittman; Mike Kohr; Mary Bailey; John Taylor; Christine Sipula; Reddick Library, Ottawa, Illinois; Larry Sheldon, New Rochelle Public Library; Glenn Longacre, The National Archives of Chicago (the repository of many records from Argonne National Laboratory); archives of the *Chicago Times, Chicago Tribune, Chicago Herald and Examiner, Ottawa Daily Republican-Times,* Ottawa's *The Daily Times* and lgrossman.com; and the Luminous Processes women I interviewed in 1978 and 1979, and those who provided other information for this book. Thanks to my wife, Janet (Saleda) Ridings, for her continued support of my work.

For further reading, especially on the New Jersey radium workers, get the books *Deadly Glow* (1999) by Ross Mullner; *The Radium Girls* (2016) by Kate Moore; and *Radium Girls* (1997) by Claudia Clark.

INTRODUCTION
"IT WILL PUT PINK CHEEKS ON YOU"

The story of the Radium Dial Company in Ottawa, Illinois, is a story of horror, tragedy, misery, and incredible callousness that extended to corporate criminal behavior.

Radium Dial opened in Ottawa in September 1922, just a few years after the company opened a plant in Orange, New Jersey. Young women took jobs at Radium Dial, applying luminous paint on clock dials to make them glow in the dark. The paint contained radium. The women were told to dip the brush made of camel's hair in the radium paint, then put the tip of the brush to their tongues, in order to get a fine point for the precise work.

Their careers as dial painters began at a high rate of pay—averaging between $17 and $42 a week, depending on the number of dials they could produce, which was a very high wage in those days. The business was located in the former Ottawa Township High School building on Columbus Street, on the southeast corner with Washington Street, one block from the park where Abraham Lincoln and Stephen A. Douglas debated in 1858. The building was built in 1879. A new high school replaced it on East Main Street in 1916.

Ottawa's facility was the largest producer of painted dials in the world by 1925, producing more than 1 million dials per year. Those early years were happy ones. The women enjoyed their work, and they enjoyed taking a little radium paint home for fun. They would paint their teeth, their fingernails, their eyelids, the buttons on their clothes, and more, to delight in seeing it all glow in the dark.

Radium was discovered in 1898 in France by Marie and Pierre Curie. Even in those early years of Radium Dial, the danger of radium was known to the educated, but it was not widely known to the general public. However, it did not take long for radium poisoning and death to appear for these Ottawa women. They could see it coming, as the newspapers started printing stories in the 1920s of the New Jersey women who were dying. Ottawa women started dying in the late 1920s.

When the New Jersey stories appeared in the newspapers, the managers in the Ottawa plant told their anxious workers that the radium paint was harmless. In fact, they said it was good for their complexion. "It will put pink cheeks on you," Rufus Reed told them. Instead, their teeth fell out, their jaws fell off, and their bones disintegrated and broke. Instead of putting pink in their cheeks, it put the women in their graves.

They were called "Ottawa's Doomed Women" and "The Society of the Living Dead." It was not just a sensational headline written by a newspaper editor. There really was a "Society of the Living Dead." The group was started in 1937 by the women dial painters in Ottawa, who recognized their own fate and who wanted to draw attention to the situation in order to help other women who were affected.

The dying women fought Radium Dial in court to get compensation to pay their medical bills and for having their lives taken at an early age. The company denied responsibility and continued to fight, even after a few women were awarded just a few hundred dollars.

As the Ottawa women started dying, and panic started setting in, the owners closed Radium Dial and opened a new plant a few blocks away under the name Luminous Processes. They told the workers that the procedures were safe, and the women believed them. The company continued its deadly work for another forty years.

Some people might think the newspapers over-sensationalized the Radium Dial workers, as seen by some of the "Doomed to Die" and "Living Dead" headlines. Some coverage was dramatic and sensationalized, but how can such a horror be overly sensationalized? The women who were suffering, and their families, did not consider it excessive.

The women formed "The Society of the Living Dead" so that the public could know the true situation and not believe the lies of the company. Some of those newspaper headlines are reprinted in this book to emphasize to a new generation that it really was as horrific as it was portrayed.

Pictures convey a message that words alone cannot. When you see a picture of Catherine Donohue collapsing and crying, "Don't leave me, Tom! Stay with me always!" you cannot help but be touched. Seeing Margaret Looney's high school picture, Charlotte Purcell's empty left sleeve, pictures of the women who were asking for a little justice for the death sentences they had been given, or when you read Gloria Boone's heartfelt words about growing up without a mother, it puts a tender human face on this story, making these women much more than just names on a page.

The story sounds unbelievable, but it is true.

1

RADIUM:
THE WONDERFUL DISCOVERY

Radium was thought to be a cure for everything, including arthritis, high blood pressure, diarrhea, constipation, impotency, and even cancer. Indeed, radium did kill cancerous tumors when properly applied by doctors in some cases. In many more cases, it killed the patient. Doctors, writers, and others waxed poetically about the wonders of radium in books, cartoons, and a variety of medicines and products.

Marie and Pierre Curie viewed their discovery with "amazement and delight." The Curies shared the 1903 Nobel Prize in Physics with Henri Becquerel, who discovered uranium. Marie Curie won the Nobel Prize in Chemistry in 1911; her daughter, Irene, won the Nobel Prize in Chemistry in 1935. The curie (a unit of radioactivity) and the element curium were named for her.

It did not take long for the dangers of radium exposure to become known. Unfortunately, the financial benefits outweighed the concerns for the safety of the people who handled it.

Radium is created by the decay of radioactive elements. Ra-226 is created by the decay of U-238 uranium. This radium is used in the medical profession, as well as in dial painting. Ra-228 is created by the decay of Th-232, thorium, a less expensive form also used in these industries.

William Hammer developed a radium paint in 1902 and was the first to apply it to clock and watch dials. Dr. Sabin von Sochocky also discovered a radium paint formula and started a company that made luminous dials, Radium Luminous Material Corporation, in 1914 with George Willis. The luminous paint was called Undark. Von Sochocky was ousted as president in a corporate takeover in 1921. The company was renamed United States Radium Corporation. Some months after his departure from the company, Dr. Willis became ill. He died in September 1922. His right thumb had been amputated; tests revealed it was riddled with cancer.

Sabin von Sochocky died in 1928 of aplastic anemia, caused by radium exposure; his teeth fell out and his fingers turned black before he died. He was forty-five. Marie Curie died in 1934 from leukemia, caused by radium exposure. William Hammer died in 1934.

Willis published the findings of his illness in the February 1923 issue of the *Journal of the American Medical Association*, writing: "The reputation for harmlessness enjoyed by radium may, after all, depend on the fact that, so far, not very many persons have been exposed to large

Above: Marie Curie and her daughter, Irene, in their Paris laboratory.

Left: Dr. Sabin von Sochocky.

Undark was a substance that could be painted on just about anything to make it glow in the dark. This ad was in the *Literary Digest* in 1920. It was made by Radium Luminous Material Corporation of New York.

amounts of radium by daily handling over long periods. There is good reason to fear that neglect of precautions may result in serious injury to the radium workers themselves."

The world's most famous health springs have always been considered curative and invigorating. Yet do not spend too much time there; they are radioactive because of radon gas, which is produced by radium in the ground where the waters flow.

That was known from the early 1900s, becoming a belief that the radioactivity caused the spring's healthy results. This was accepted in the highest circles. Professor Bertram Boltwood of Yale believed radioactivity was "carrying electrical energy into the depths of the body, subjecting the juices, protoplasm, and nuclei of the cells to an immediate bombardment by explosions of electrical atoms." He said it stimulated "cell activity, arousing all secretory and excretory organs, causing the system to throw off waste products," and it was "an agent for the destruction of bacteria."

A number of products were made to satisfy the public need. If you had a disease or any kind of ailment, drinking Radithor would cure it. It was "guaranteed harmless in every respect." It was claimed to cure anemia, angina, arthritis, arteriosclerosis, asthma, diabetes, epilepsy, heart disease, high blood pressure, hyper/hypo thyroid, hysteria, kidney disease, menopause, obesity, rheumatism, senility, sexual decline, sinus conditions, skin disorders, wrinkles, and much more.

The Radium Ore Revigator Company's jar was made of radium ore. The user was instructed to fill the jar with water every night and drink six or more glasses daily. It promised a cure for a dozen ailments, including anemia, asthma, stiff joints, high blood pressure, arthritis, apoplexy, bronchitis, inflammation of the bladder, diabetes, eczema, gout, laryngitis, lumbago, inflammation of the uterus, and much more.

Other radium water devices—all which claimed to cure the above ailments and more—were the Radium Emanator, Radium Vitalizer Health Fount Jar, and the Lifetime Radium Vitalizer. Dr. Saubermann's Radium Therapy Jar claimed, "It continuously emits radium emanation at a fixed rate and keeps the water in the jar always charged to a fixed and measurable strength."

Hogan Radio-Active Ore was placed in drinking water to cure a dozen ailments. Lifetime Radium-Vitalizer Water Jar "aids nature by increasing the number of and building up the red corpuscles of the blood. It eliminates poisons from the system, causing the best of digestion of your food."

Sleepy Water was claimed to restore natural health balance by neutralizing the unhealthy or diseased condition of acidity in the body with its slightly alkaline nature. The water was bottled from a spring in Hot Springs, Arkansas. Ra-tor Radium Mineral Water claimed it was "a natural product brought to you straight from the treasure vault of Nature."

A number of radium products claimed to cure sexual dysfunction. Vita Radium Suppositories claimed it was a "tone restorer for sex, and energizers for the entire nervous, glandular, and circulatory systems. The radium is absorbed through the walls of the lower colon, enters the blood stream and is carried to all parts of the body, to the weakened organs that need its vitalizing aid. After leaving its durable healthy results, the radium is gradually eliminated in about three days." It was "guaranteed entirely harmless."

RADIUM
EMANATION WATER
Drives Out Uric Acid

Suffering from too much uric acid and diseases caused by faulty elimination—**Rheumatism, Gout, Periodical Headaches, Neuralgia, Constipation, Neurasthenia, Auto-Intoxication and Lack of Bodily Vigor**—quickly relieved in a natural way without drugs or chemicals by our new discovery

THE WAY TO MAKE RADIUM WATER IN YOUR OWN HOME

with our Rayode. A little device containing Radium enough to supply 2,700 Mache Units of Radio-activity, in two quarts of water every twenty-four hours, for less than 10c a day. The Rayode will last a lifetime.

SEND FOR FREE LITERATURE

Tells how you can buy or rent a Rayode to make Radium Water in your own home, with your own ordinary drinking water. Address:

THE COLORADO RADIUM PRODUCTS COMPANY
635 First National Bank Building   Denver, Colo

X-RADIUM MFG. CO.

DISTRIBUTORS OF

HOUSEHOLD
ARTICLES

FROM FACTORY
TO FAMILY DIRECT

VALUABLE
PREMIUMS

—FREE—

103 DUDLEY ST., BOSTON

ARE YOU RUN DOWN?

Radium may give you more benefit than anything else known. It is a great tonic and stimulant.

Nuradium   Tablets contain radium and each tablet is a mine of powerful, penetrating energy for stomach, muscles, nerves, mind and entire system.

Specially priced, $1.39   *Try Them*

A few of the odd radium products from the early twentieth century.

Le Rouge à Lèvres sain
Rouge à Lèvres THO-RADIA
ORANGÉ . FEU . VIF . MOYEN . FONCÉ .
ETUI COMPLET : 16! . RECHANGE : 8!
EN PHARMACIE SEULEMENT

RADIUM v. GREY HAIR
Who'd Dream she was 50?
50—and not a grey hair to be seen. Wonderful! Yet an absolute fact. Let 'CARADIUM' do for you what it has done for thousands of our clients in all parts of the world. 'CARADIUM' will quickly restore, right from the hair roots, the natural colour, health and beauty to your hair, making you look 10 to 20 years younger.
Write for Free Hair Book.
'Caradium' is NOT A DYE
CONTAINING RADIO-ACTIVE WATER
Regular application of 'Caradium' will revivify the colour glands of the hair and cause the natural pigment to flow afresh. 'Caradium' Restorer is just as efficacious in cases of premature or inherited greyness or greyness caused by illness, worry, or overwork. It is absolutely sure. So natural is the course of restoration, that the use of 'Caradium' is absolutely undetectable.
Grey Hair will never appear if CARADIUM IS USED ONCE WEEKLY AS A TONIC
Caradium Shampoo Powders (for dry or Greasy hair) are the finest in the world for producing Soft and Glossy hair, 6d. each, Packets of twelve, 5/-
WARNING.—Ask for Caradium Regd. and see that you get it; imitations are useless.
Caradium REGD.
A 4/- size is now available for those only slightly grey. 'Caradium' Hair Restorer is obtainable of all good Chemists, Harrods, Whiteleys, Barkers, Selfridge's, Timothy Whites, Boots, Taylor's Drug Stores, etc., or direct in plain wrapper, POST FREE U.K. (overseas postage 2/6 extra) from :—
Large Size
4/-
7/6
'CARADIUM' REGD., 38 Great Smith Street, Westminster, London.

Our New Radium $5.00 Permanent Wave Beauty
COPYRIGHT 1924
R.W. CHERRY

X-Radium Heater
A little marvel of comfort and economy wanted in every home
The X-Radium Heater is, in reality, a neat little stove, four inches high and seven inches in diameter. Gives heat without consuming fuel. Made in two parts: first, a heating pad of stamped steel filled with X-Radium (a chemical substance recently discovered possessing the same affinity for heat that a sponge has for water) ; second, a stamped steel bowl-shaped stand with asbestos mat in the bottom, into which the pad is placed after being heated. Finely finished, polished and heavily nickel-plated.
No extra cost in heating the X-Radium Heater. Set the pad on the stove or range (coal, wood, gas, gasoline or oil) and in twenty minutes it will be hot and keeps hot for two hours.
Keeps the coffee, soup, vegetables, meat and pastry hot, keeps the flat-irons hot, keeps anything hot. Takes the place of the hot water bag and is the greatest foot warmer on earth. Will last a lifetime. It is everybody's necessity and everybody can have it. Price only $2.50 (East of Missouri River).
Our Free Trial Offer.—Order the X-Radium Heater through your local dealer. We will send it to him, transportation prepaid, and instruct him to allow you to try it for ten days. If satisfactory pay him $2.50. If you are not satisfied, return it to the dealer. You have no risk in the matter. This trial offer shows our confidence in the merits of the X-Radium Heater. So please have no hesitation in taking advantage of it.
Novelty Manufacturing Company, Department B.
JACKSON, MICHIGAN, U. S. A.

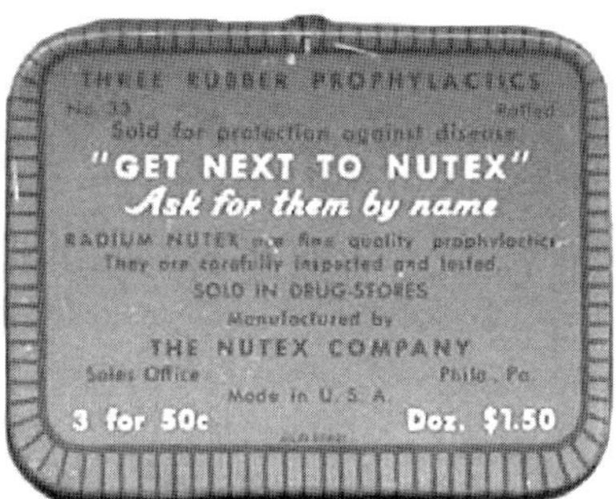

Radium Is Restoring *HEALTH* to Thousands

No medicine or drugs. Just a light, small, comfortable inexpensive Radio-Active Pad, worn on the back by day and over the stomach at night. Sold on trial. You can be sure it is helping you before you buy it. Over 150,000 sold on this plan. Thousands have written us that it healed them of Neuritis, Rheumatism, High Blood Pressure, Constipation, Nervous Prostration, Asthma and other respiratory disorders, Heart, Liver, Kidney and Bladder trouble, etc. No matter what you have tried, or what your trouble may be, try Degnen's Radio-Active Solar Pad at our risk. Write today for Trial offer and descriptive literature.

RADIUM APPLIANCE CO.
(Established 1916)
2103 Bradbury Building   Los Angeles, Calif.

Nu-Man Gland Tablets and Vagatone Gland Tablets claimed: To] restore sexual power and endurance to men who have been weakened by excesses and loss of vital fluids. Brings back pep and vitality and can be expected to stop involuntary night emissions when due to lack of sex tone. It is recommended for the purpose of increasing the number of red corpuscles in the blood and thereby raising the individual's vitality and his resistance to colds, other sickness, and cold weather. It will remedy sexual apathy or indifference due to low glandular activity. Testone Radium Appliance and Suspensory was a rubber envelope with radium salts to be wrapped around the testicles to provide energizing gamma rays to the testes. Soothol Radium Bougies was soluble radium salts in a gelatin base, inserted into the urethral canal. It was claimed to "stop premature ejaculation due to inflamed, congested or irritated condition of the urethral canal and prostate gland resulting from excessive indulgences, venereal infection or injurious habits; stops stricture making it easier to pass urine."

Degnen's Standard Radioactive Solar Pad was to be charged in the sun and then applied to the body, where it discharged "energy into the system, sending life-giving current through the blood and nervous system." Farnsworth Colloidal was ampoules of radium, claimed to cure cancers and ulcerative conditions. Gable Ionic Charger was a cylinder connected to a tube with a large squeeze bulb, which inserted radium water.

Arium Radium Tablets claimed, "Radium ends agony of rheumatism, neuritis, neuralgia and gout" and "reduces inflammation, relieves pain, and renews the energy and vigor of youth." Paradox Radium Liquid X-Ray "breaks down and destroys disease cells. Accelerates healthy tissue, expands capillaries and dissipates congestion." Paradox Radium Ointment "destroys deep-seated, abnormal cells and promotes rapid, normal development." Radio-endocrinator contained radium-soaked paper, placed over the endocrine glands; it "improved looks, character and memory." Radio-Sulpho Brew came in a poultice, ointment, salve, and more as a "home cure for cancer or malignant disease," and was sold "for treatment to the white race only."

Radio-X Greaseless Cream was used for treatment of pimples, blackheads, freckles, sunburn, oily skin and blemishes. Radium Face Clay was from Czechoslovakia, used for the same conditions. Radium Mountain Water came from Radium Cave Spring in Arkansas and was used for high blood pressure, rheumatism, kidney disorders, and other chronic conditions.

Charles Howell of Hull, Illinois, was nothing more than a quack medicine man. He marketed Dr. Howell's Harmless Radium Pile Cure, Dr. Howell's Harmless Radium Remedy for Enlarged Prostate Glands, and Dr. Howell's Radium Cure for Deafness and Head Noises—all of which claimed guaranteed cures.

There was radium candy, cosmetics, and more. Radium Chocolate was made in Germany in the 1930s. Dormand Toothpaste was made in Germany from 1941 to 1945. Radium Emanation Bath Salts were good for nervous disorders, insomnia, general debility, arthritis, and rheumatism. Radium Bread contained water from St. Joachimstahl, with a small amount of radium.

Tho-Radia products included face powder, skin cream, lipstick, rouge, and toothpaste. It claimed to activate circulation, tone and firm tissues, eliminate fat, and suppress wrinkles. It contained both radium and thorium, making it especially deadly. The company also produced Neothorium for the "intimate daily hygiene for women."

Radium Fertilizer claimed to increase vegetables in size by thirty-nine percent, and to make lawns and shrubbery flourish. Endless Refrigerator/Freezer Deodorizer was made in Japan in the 1980s. It was a green plastic "honeycomb," which claimed to destroy odors for years by emitting natural negative ions which neutralized odor-causing positive ions inside the refrigerator. The Lifestone Cigarette Holder was sold until the 1960s, with the promise it would "protect users from lung cancer, promise them beautiful faces, and excellent health."

There were a number of products with "radium" in the name which did not contain radium; the makers only wanted to be part of the radium craze, before the dangers were known. There was Radium Beer, Radium Boot Polish, Radium Butter, Radium Clippers, Radium Cigarettes, Radium Cigars, Radium Cleanser, Radium Enamel, Radium Leather Dye, Radium Lump Gloss Starch, even Radium Playing Cards, Radium Razor Blades, and Radium Condoms. Also, of course, there were radium clocks and wristwatches.

Standard Chemical's ad in the June 1916 issue of the journal *Radium.*

Radium Baths at the Hotel Will Rogers, Claremore, Oklahoma.

RADIUM SPRAY
THE NEW
Combination Bug Killer, Disinfect-ant and Furniture Polish

Guaranteed by Grocers and Druggists
to Kill All Insects and Vermin

TRY IT AT OUR EXPENSE

MANUFACTURED BY
RADIUM SPRAY CO., Inc.

114 THIRD AVE. SOUTH   **SEATTLE, WASHINGTON**

It killed bugs and polished your furniture.

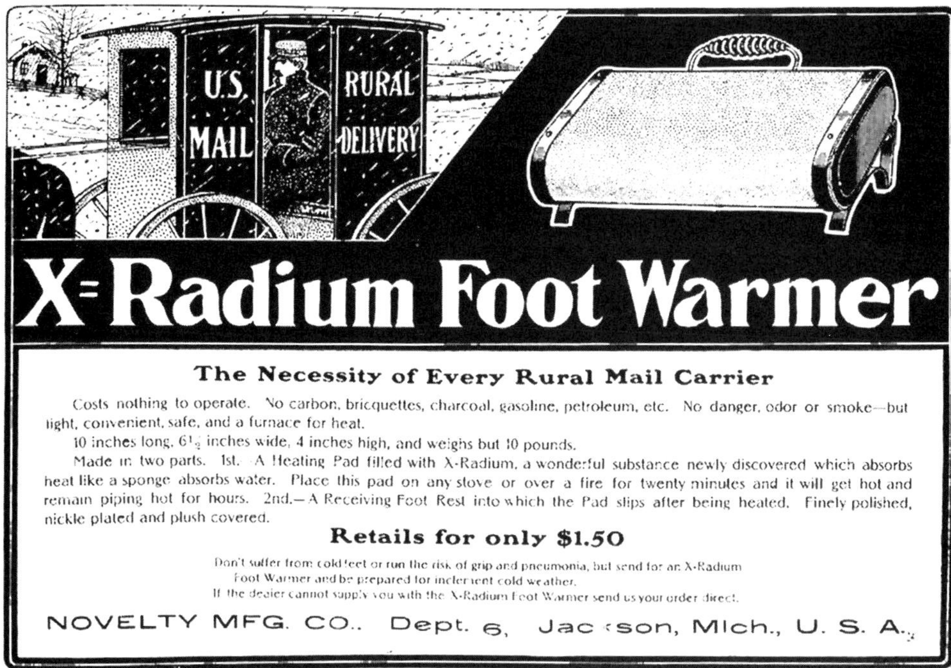

Radium Baths at the Hotel Will Rogers, Claremore, Oklahoma.

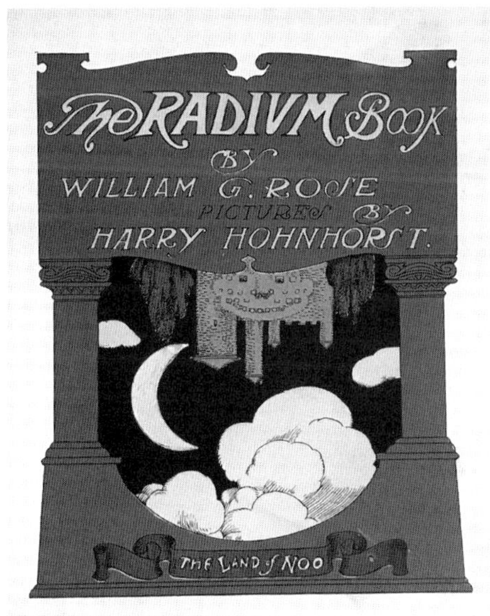

The Radium Book, by William G. Rose, with illustrations by Harry Hohnhorst, was published for children in 1905, when radium was a new and marvelous discovery. The first page instructs readers to hold each full-page picture to a light in the window, or a gas or electric light, and then look at it glow in the dark. The story is very like *The Wizard of Oz*, with a character named Dorothy traveling to the Land of Noo and meeting many Oz-like characters.

The Charleston Radium Show played the Luna Theatre in Kankakee, Illinois, in August 1925, as part of a traveling vaudeville circuit.

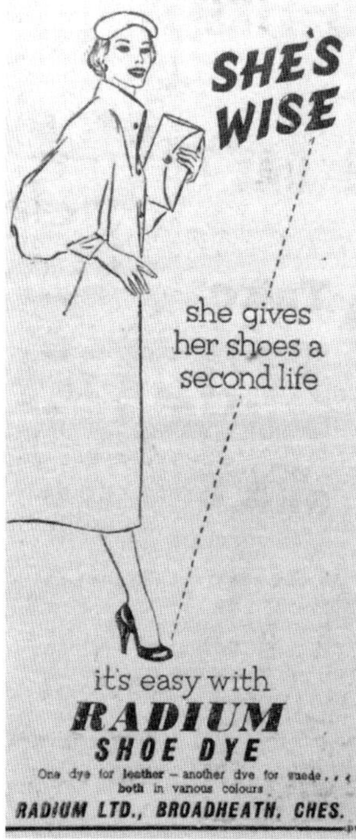

Winsor McCay, an acclaimed cartoonist best known for *Little Nemo in Slumberland*, was among those hailing radium in this 1914 drawing. It was a time when it was hoped that radium would cure most anything.

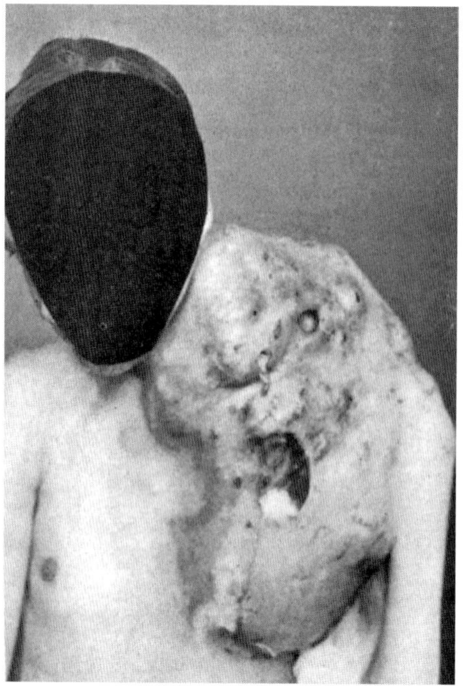 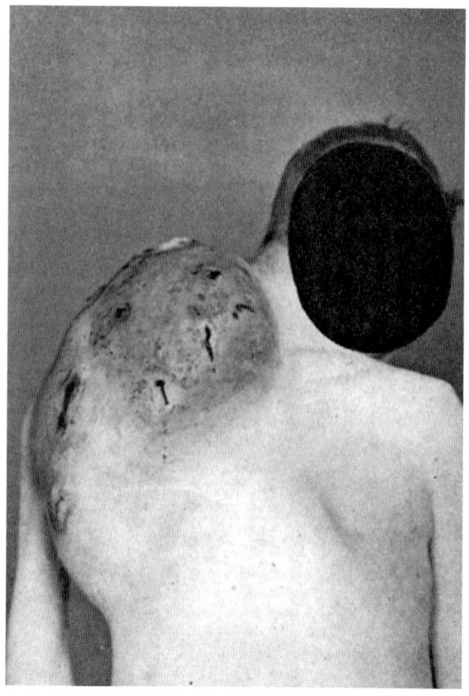

Not all was wonderful. This picture of a man with a massive tumor comes from a 1914 U.S. Senate hearing on the use of radium fertilizer.

2

RADIUM DIAL COMPANY

Radium Dial Company came out of a company started by the Flannery brothers. James and Joseph Flannery began, ironically, as undertakers in Pittsburgh, Pennsylvania. They started a company producing a new bolt for locomotives in 1904. From there, they went into mining in order to get the ore for manufacturing. Their alloy of vanadium and steel was bought by Henry Ford for his Model-T cars.

When their sister was dying of cancer in 1910, the Flannery brothers sought a cure using radium. She died, but the brothers vowed to continue looking for a cure. They founded Standard Chemical Company in 1911 and continued mining to extract radium.

Joseph Kelly, Sr.

Refined ore from Standard's mines near Uravan, Colorado, was sent to its reduction mill in Canonsburg, south of Pittsburgh, and eventually to Standard's refining laboratory in the Vanadium Building in Pittsburgh. Many years later, it was discovered that the building had high levels of radioactivity. It was decontaminated in 2002. James and Joseph Flannery both died in 1920. Joseph was fifty-two, James was sixty-five.

Joseph A. Kelly, Sr., was on the board of directors of Standard Chemical Company. Other historical accounts say that Kelly was Joseph Flannery's son-in-law. However, Kelly was married to Katherine Manning, the daughter of John Manning. Joseph Flannery was married to Mary "Mollie" Gearing, the sister of Thomas Gearing. This allowed Thomas Gearing to eventually climb to the top of the corporation. Joseph A. Kelly, Sr., started Radium Dial Company. Joseph Kelly, Jr., followed in his father's footsteps.

Standard Chemical formed a subsidiary, Radium Chemical Company, in 1913 for the marketing of radium. Radium Dial began making luminescent dials in Chicago in 1918. Its first location was at 327 N. Wells Street. By 1921, it had moved to 54 Lake Street. Yearly sales of radio-luminescent watches and clocks went from 8,500 in 1913 to 4 million in 1920.

James Flannery.

Joseph Flannery.

Since most of the dials went to Westclox in Peru, Illinois, Westclox asked Radium Dial to relocate from Chicago to Peru, which it did in 1920. Two years later, the dial factory was moved to nearby Ottawa, after Westclox complained that Radium Dial was stealing too many employees with its higher wages. At its peak, Radium Dial in Ottawa produced 1 million dials a year, the most in the United States.

Joseph Kelly, Senior and Junior, were men of mystery. They avoided prosecution, they avoided paying compensation to the people they killed and damaged, and they avoided having to pay to clean up the pieces of the planet they poisoned. They also were mysterious in leaving few footprints during their lifetimes, and after.

Joseph Kelly, Sr.'s obituary was in very few newspapers and it was brief—unusual for such a prominent man. His obituary in the *New York Daily News*, where he lived and where his company was headquartered, was two sentences. It said where and when a requiem mass would be held, and it said he was chairman of Radium Chemical Company, "which manufactured some essential parts for the first atom bombs in World War II." That was it. His obituary in the *Pittsburgh Press*, his birthplace and where he and his family are buried, was one sentence: "Joseph A. Kelly, 80, an importer of radium who worked on the first atomic bomb, in New York."

Here is what we have been able to find about the Kellys. Joseph Anthony Kelly, Sr., was born on July 29, 1884 in Pennsylvania, the son of John and Mary (Horan) Kelly. His father was a saloon keeper who was born in Wales in 1858. His father died in 1935; his mother died in 1916. John and Mary Kelly had four other children: John Kelly (1890–1952), Ellen Kelly (1895–1937), Mary Aquinas Kelly (1899–1964), and Richard Kelly (1902–1947).

The 1910 Census shows Joseph Kelly, Sr., was living in Pittsburgh and was a clerk for the railroad. Joseph Kelly married Katherine Manning on September 1, 1913, in Pittsburgh. Katherine was born in 1886 and died in 1982. Joseph and Katherine Kelly had four children: Joseph Kelly, Jr., Mollie Bergesch (1917–1998), Katherine "Cass" Armistead (1926–2013), and Anne Hemphill.

GIRLS.

No experience necessary. Those desirous of advancement can find remunerative and permanent employment here; will teach you the method of painting watch dials and pay you while learning. Experienced girls earn from $25 to $30 per wk. Large, airy studio in the loop and short hours. Apply
RADIUM DIAL CO.,
327 N. Wells-st.

GIRLS—SEVERAL—
FOR APPLYING LUMINOUS COMPOUND TO DIALS. EXPERIENCE UNNECESSARY. SALARY WHILE LEARNING. THEN VERY LIBERAL PIECE RATE. PLEASANT AND PERMANENT EMPLOYMENT.
RADIUM DIAL CO.,
327 N. WELLS-ST.

BOY—FOR LIGHT ERRAND work. RADIUM DIAL CO., 327 N. Wells-st.

GIRLS—FOR SMALL BRUSH WORK. CHINA PAINTERS PREFERRED; VERY PLEASANT WORK AND GOOD PAY.
RADIUM DIAL CO.,
54 W. LAKE-ST.

Help wanted ads from 1918 to 1920.

Above: These are dial painters at the Peru facility of Radium Dial. Boxes of clock faces are at their sides.

Left: Joseph Kelly, Sr.—1915 passport photo.

Joseph Kelly, Sr., described himself on his 1914 passport as being 6 feet tall, with a slightly receding hairline, blue eyes, brown hair, a fair complexion, and a prominent nose and chin. His address was the Vanadium Building in Pittsburgh. His passport a year later was changed to a straight nose and a smooth chin. His address changed to the Vanderbilt Hotel in New York.

Joseph Kelly, Sr., met with President Franklin D. Roosevelt and physicist Albert Einstein during World War II. Dials that glowed in the dark were needed for aircraft and ships during wartime. The company also provided the government with a processed form of radium used to detonate atomic bombs. Kelly received a citation from the government for his contribution to the war effort.

Joseph Kelly, Sr., died on May 22, 1965, in his home on Fifth Avenue in New York. He was eighty years old. His work at Radium Dial and his contribution to the war effort is basically all the public knows about him. It seems he wanted it that way.

Joseph Kelly, Jr., was born on October 13, 1918, in Pittsburgh. The 1940 Census lists him as an insurance salesman, living at home with his parents. He served in the Army Air Corps during World War II. He apparently never married. Joseph Kelly, Jr. succeeded his father as head of Radium Dial, retiring in 1989. He died on March 1, 1993.

The Kellys even pulled dirty tricks on their own business partners. Joseph Kelly, Sr., and Thomas Gearing founded Radium Chemical Company, another subsidiary, in 1936 (to avoid financial liability caused by Radium Dial). Each man owned half the stock. The company had three directors: Kelly, Gearing, and company secretary Margaret Lee. Gearing died in 1952 and his daughter, Mary Meacham, was chosen to take his place on the board. In 1955, the number of directors

The uranium mine in Uravan, Colorado, where the ore was mined for radium.

was increased to four, with Joseph Kelly, Jr., added. Lee resigned in 1961. Mrs. Meacham wanted her husband to take Lee's place, but the Kellys installed Julian Hemphill (son-in-law of Joseph Kelly, Sr.) instead. The Gearing family took Radium Chemical to court in 1961. Among the allegations were that the Kellys added people to the board of directors in violation of by-laws and agreements; that the company was paying Kelly family members excessive amounts; that a senile and crippled Joseph Kelly, Sr., was made chairman of the board to be paid a large salary for doing nothing; that Charles Bergesch (another Kelly son-in-law) was being paid a high salary for doing nothing; and that the company was hiding assets to defraud the Gearings. The courts ruled in favor of the Kellys.

Joseph Kelly, Sr.

The Kellys knew the dangers of handling radium and yet they provided no safety precautions in the workplace. Instead of at least warning the women, so they could take their own precautions, the Kellys lied to them and said radium was not harmful. They paid doctors to lie to the women, as these workers continued to ingest radium. They hired teams of lawyers to fight claims in the courts and they left the taxpayers to pay for countless millions of dollars to clean up their messes across the country, all while hiding in their Fifth Avenue apartment in New York. Joseph A. Kelly, Senior and Junior, may be considered among the worst corporate criminals in American history.

Katherine Kelly.

The Kellys, Flannerys, and Gearings had one thing in common with most of their radium victims: they all were Catholic.

Above: Joseph A. Kelly, Sr.'s draft registration card for World War I, in September 1918.

Next page: Joseph Kelly's letter to apply for a passport, May 10, 1915. Before he listed his address as the Vanderbilt Hotel in New York, he had listed it as The Vanadium Building in Pittsburgh. The Vanadium Building was renamed the Flannery Building; today, it is the Parkvale Building.

Cable Address "Radium" Pittsburgh Pa

Radium Chemical Company

Producers and Distributors of

Radium and Radium Preparations

Offices and Laboratories

Forbes and Meyran Avenues

Department of Sales

Pittsburgh, Pa.

May
Tenth
Nineteen Fifteen

Department of State,

    Bureau of Citizenship,

       Washington, D. C.

Gentlemen:-

    Enclosed please find application for passport, which kindly grant and mail to the writer care of the Vanderbilt Hotel, New York. As I have booked passage on the American Liner S. S. "St. Louis", sailing from New York, Saturday, May 15th, will appreciate it very much if you will give this matter your usual prompt attention and see that the passport reaches New York not later than Friday, May 14th.

    I am returning herewith for cancellation, passport No. 39954, issued to the writer August 25th, 1914.

    The object of my trip to England is in connection with our Radium business and I anticipate being away at least two months.

    Thanking you in advance, I am,

    Respectfully yours,

PRESIDENT.

3

THE NEW JERSEY
AND CONNECTICUT
RADIUM WOMEN

The same thing that would happen in Ottawa started in Orange, New Jersey, and in Waterbury, Connecticut, the sites of other Radium Dial plants.

Amelia Maggia was the first to die, in 1922. Amelia started work in New Jersey in 1917, at the age of twenty. Her sisters, Albina and Quinta, also worked in the New Jersey plant. Albina and Quinta left in 1919 to get married and raise families.

Amelia began having health problems in 1921. She had to quit work the following year. Her jaw disintegrated, her teeth fell out, she had a large abscess in her ears, and she suffered horrible pain before dying on September 12, 1922 at the age of twenty-five.

Her dentist questioned Radium Dial officials; they rebuffed him and refused to cooperate. The dentist treated other radium workers and found the same condition. Meanwhile, the company had Amelia's cause of death listed as syphilis and quickly had her buried. An autopsy in 1927 found that her bones were highly radioactive. The same radium poisoning later killed the other Maggia sisters.

Irene Rudolph painted dials for two and a half years, from 1918 to 1921. Her health problems began in 1922. She suffered horribly until her death in 1923 at the age of twenty-one. However, it was accusations by her dentists against the company that led managers in Orange to tell their workers to stop putting the brushes in their mouths.

Hazel Kuser died on December 9, 1924, at the age of twenty-five. She started work at the age of sixteen and left after five years to marry her childhood sweetheart, Theodore. Six months after their wedding, she started feeling the effects of the radium. For four and a half years, she suffered terrible pain. She had to be drugged in her last few months because the pain was so great.

Frances Splettscher died in 1925. She was just seventeen when she went to work in 1921 in the Waterbury plant. Her story was similar to other workers. Her teeth rotted and part of her jaw came out when a dentist pulled a tooth.

Radium Dial hired a fraudulent "doctor" named Frederick Flinn in 1925 to examine the women at Waterbury. He told them they were all right. Flinn was not a doctor, but he made a career covering up for radium companies, which included testifying against the women in court.

A drawing from *The American Weekly* in 1926 that was reprinted across the country.

Above: The New Jersey dial painting plant.

Right: Carefree New Jersey dial painters, before they started dying.

When radium poisoning finally could not be denied, he convinced some of the women to take small settlements without consulting a lawyer. One victim received $43.75.

Cecil Drinker, a Harvard University physiology professor, studied the Radium Dial situation in 1924 and found a contaminated workplace and radium in the blood of the workers and cancers in young female employees. He found the women's hair, faces, hands, necks, arms, clothes, and even their underwear all glowed. Mr. Drinker found that the chemists in the laboratories had no contamination because lead screens, masks, and tongs were used.

Edward Lehman, a Radium Dial chemist who had lesions on his hands, was confronted by Mr. Drinker during the investigation. Mr. Lehman said he was not worried. Mr. Drinker testified, "This attitude was characteristic of those in authority throughout the plant. There seemed to be an utter lack of realization of the dangers inherent in the material which was being manufactured." Mr. Lehman was dead within the year.

U.S. Radium president Arthur Roeder disputed Mr. Drinker's findings, and even threatened a lawsuit to prevent it from being published. Mr. Roeder also threatened others whose studies came to similar conclusions.

Sarah Maillefer died on June 18, 1925, at the age of thirty-five. She was a single mother who started working at the age of twenty-eight. Her body was sent to California to be examined by Dr. Robert A. Milliken, winner of the 1923 Nobel Prize for Physics. Sarah was the first dial painter to be tested for radium poisoning, and she was the first victim to be autopsied.

A small article in the *New Jersey Journal* on June 29, 1925, speculated that Sarah's death could have been "radium necrosis, which has killed and stricken a number of other New Jersey dial painters." The story said the teeth and gums of the women were afflicted, caused by putting the brush in the mouth. It also said, "A representative of one company reports that he sees no reason why the paint used would have any destructive effect."

Sarah Maillefer was the seventh New Jersey dial painter to die. Her death came ten days after Edward Lehman's death. Sarah worked alongside her sister, Marguerite Carlough. Marguerite, who in 1925 was the first New Jersey victim to file a lawsuit, died on December 26, 1926 at the age of twenty-five.

Marguerite's lawsuit caused the Waterbury Clock Company to stop their dial painters from putting the tips of their brushes to their mouths.

Grace Fryer noticed that when she blew her nose, her handkerchief glowed in the dark. She and other women in New Jersey amused themselves by painting their teeth, fingernails, and more, so they would glow in the dark.

Grace worked there from 1917 to 1920. She told a newspaper reporter in 1928 that the women were told to put the brushes to their mouths to maintain a fine point, and that she did so about six times for every dial. Two years after she left Radium Dial, Grace's teeth started falling out and her jaw developed an abscess. She continued working, but she needed to wear a steel brace because her spine had collapsed.

Radium Dial doctors and public relations men tried to spin the condition of Grace and other female employees into ulcers, syphilis, and other ailments—anything but

Grace Fryer.

Popular Science
MONTHLY

JULY, 1929 | **SUMNER BLOSSOM** *Editor* | VOL. 115, NO. 1

IF YOUR doctor should give you only one year to live, what would you do? That's the situation these five girls faced a year ago. Twelve months have passed, and they're still smiling. This intensely human article tells why. Left to right are: Mrs. Quinta McDonald, Mrs. Edna Hussman, Mrs. Albina Larice, Miss Katherine Schaub, Miss Grace Fryer.

Doomed to Die—and They Live!

Medical Science Brings a Ray of Hope Into the Tragic Lives of Five Girls Poisoned by Radium

By ROBERT E. MARTIN

A FEW weeks ago, two of the five New Jersey girls who are believed to be slowly dying from radium poisoning they contracted while painting luminous watch dials were taken to the Memorial Hospital in New York City and subjected to an entirely new course of treatment. An almost impenetrable cloak of mystery was thrown over the proceedings. Hospital officials refused all information, and the doctors in charge declined to reveal the nature of the attempted cure and of the effects they expected from it.

But through this screen of professional secrecy, one fact stood out with the cheery brightness of a beacon amid utter darkness. That was that the board of distinguished physicians who, for about a year, have been studying the cases of the five women, have not relinquished all hope of remedying their strange and terrible disease.

Slight as this hope may be, it gains some strength if considered with other developments in the stirring tragedy. It is now just a year since each of the young women received a $10,000 compensation in cash and a pension of $600 annually for "life" from the radium company which had employed them. At that time, the medical profession predicted that they had but one year to live. The twelve months have passed. All of the five girls are alive and doctors declare their condition is only "a little worse" than in June, 1928.

When medical science passed sentence on the patients, their lingering ailment was diagnosed as "radium necrosis." Necrosis means mortification or death. In other words, it was supposed that the bones and blood-making centers of the young women were dying as a result of the activity of the radium their systems had absorbed. In the face of this sinister and unknown disease, medicine was virtually impotent.

But now it appears that science has made a second guess. The cause of the girls' dreadful suffering may, after all, not be radium, but mesothorium, another radioactive substance. Radium is insoluble and loses half of its potency in 1,750 years! Mesothorium, however, is not only soluble, so that it can be gradually eliminated from the human body, but half of its strength is dissipated in six and seven tenths years. Thus, if the mesothorium theory proves correct, the doomed women, whose first symptoms appeared about 1925, will be "reprieved" in a couple of years and, though broken in health or crippled, may live to a ripe old age!

THIS amazing human drama, which may end tragically or comparatively happily, opened about twelve years ago. It was war time. The five young women, now either in their late twenties or early thirties, then between fifteen and twenty years old, were part of a group of some hundred light-hearted girls employed by the United States Radium Corporation at

Popular Science magazine did a story on the New Jersey dial painters in July 1929, and they got it all wrong. They gave the dying women hope by claiming they would recover because their illness was not caused by radium but by mesothorium, which it somehow deemed less harmful. The five "smiling" women in the picture all died of radium poisoning, the first one dying a few months after this story was published.

radium poisoning, even though later investigations proved that the company knew for sure it was radium poisoning.

However, they could not hide the truth for long. Consumer advocates, medical investigators, and even journalists made the connection to radium, which was the common thread in all the cases. Radium goes to the bone, which explained why the women's jaws were crumbling and why they lost teeth and had cancers of the bone.

Dr. Harrison Martland, medical examiner of Essex County, New Jersey, conducted studies that proved in 1925 that radium poisoning killed the dial painters. He published an eighty-two-page article in the October 1931 issue of *The American Journal of Cancer* that left no doubt. It contained many graphic pictures (it is still available online). The publicity about the dying women caused Radium Dial to close its Orange plant in 1926.

Grace Fryer sued Radium Dial, even though it took two years to find a lawyer brave enough to take her case. The lawsuit was filed in 1927, with four other women joining: Katherine Schaub, Edna Hussman, Quinta McDonald, and Albina Larice. The newspapers called them "The Five Doomed Women." Katherine was fifteen when she went to work in the Orange dial plant. Edna was sixteen. Grace was eighteen.

This picture from the *Popular Science* article in 1929, colored in an eerie green, was captioned: "As Mrs. Hussman caught sight of herself in the mirror, she screamed and fell in a dead faint. In the dark room, the mirror reflected a ghostly light radiating from her body, and her face and hair were weirdly luminous."

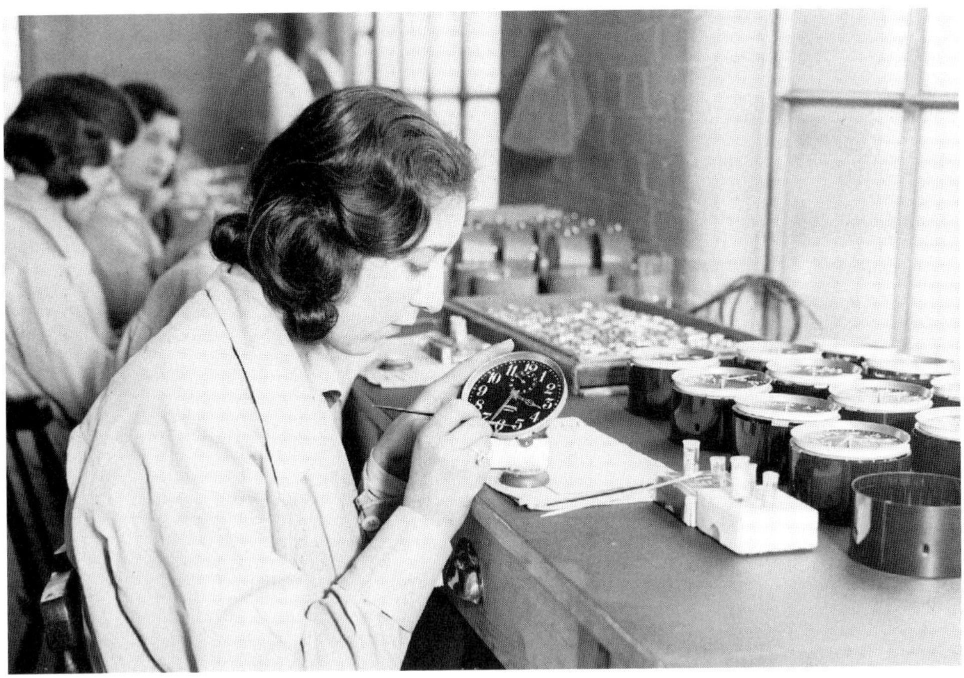

Painting dials for the Ingersoll Watch Company in Waterbury, Connecticut, in 1932.

New Jersey dial painters.

The same thing happened in New Jersey and in Ottawa—the women could not find a lawyer who would stand up to the big corporation. Finally, in 1927, Raymond Berry took the cases of the New Jersey women.

By the time the New Jersey lawsuit came to court in 1928, the five "Radium Girls" were unable to raise their arms to take the oath. The testimony from the women about their horrible pain shocked newspaper readers.

Radium Dial lawyers used delaying tactics in court, obtaining continuances, hoping the witnesses would die before more could testify. However, crusading journalists, particularly *New York World* editor Walter Lippman, made the issue so hot that the court agreed to an earlier hearing. Just a few days before the trial was to start, Radium Dial settled out of court, admitting no liability but agreeing to pay each of the defendants $10,000 and $600 a year for every year they lived, and to pay medical expenses.

Quinta Maggia McDonald died in 1929 at the age of twenty-nine, seven years after her sister Amelia. Grace Fryer and Katherine Schaub died in 1933, at the ages of thirty-four and thirty, respectively. Edna Hussman died in 1939 at age thirty-seven. Albina (Maggia) Larice died in 1946. All of these women died in their thirties, except Albina, who was fifty-one when she died. Florence Casler of New Jersey died in 1951.

Grace Fryer told *Popular Science* magazine in July 1929 that she did not spend any of her $10,000 settlement. She said it was "safely invested for the future." Unfortunately, the stock market crashed three months later.

The number of cases of horrible cancers fell dramatically after 1925 when dial painters were ordered to not put the brushes to their mouths. However, the cases of women who learned this too late continued into the late 1930s. Cases of radium poisoning continued as long as radium was used.

The company, later called Radium Chemical, did the same denial and stonewalling in New Jersey and New York as it did in Ottawa. As state officials tried to get the company to clean up its properties in the 1980s and 1990s, Radium Chemical evaded and eventually skipped out, leaving taxpayers to foot the bill. New York investigators found that the owner, Joseph A. Kelly, Jr., did the same thing in Ottawa, Illinois, and in Athens, Georgia. The studies, investigations, and publicity in New Jersey helped in the cases of the Ottawa workers.

In 1979, the U.S. Environmental Protection Agency found levels of radioactivity twenty times higher than was safe at the dial-painting building in Orange and at landfills where the company had dumped radioactive waste. About 750 homes built on top of the waste, on 200 acres of land, had to be decontaminated. The EPA ordered the corporate successor of Radium Dial to do the cleanup, but that did not happen. The New Jersey Supreme Court in 1991 found Radium Dial "forever liable" and said the company had "constructive knowledge" of the dangers of its business.

It was not just the "Radium Girls" in Ottawa, New Jersey, and Connecticut who were dying. The world took note when one of the nation's most prominent men died of radium poisoning. Eben MacBurney Byers was a very wealthy industrialist, socialite, and championship golfer from Pittsburgh. Byers injured his arm in 1927, and Dr. Charles Moyar prescribed Radithor, spurred by a 17-percent kickback on every bottle the doctor sold.

Radithor was a mixture of distilled water, radium, and mesothorium. It was made by Bailey Radium Laboratories of East Orange, New Jersey, from 1925 to 1930. The company claimed Radithor could cure a hundred illnesses.

The owner, William Bailey, was not a doctor and had no medical training. He had been in trouble with the law and had served time in prison for various frauds, especially for fake cures. Bailey was a con man, taking advantage of the radium craze, in a time before the public knew the dangers.

Eben Byers believed the tonic was working. He began drinking three bottles of Radithor a day. By late 1930, after having drank approximately 1,400 two-ounce bottles of Radithor, Byers began to feel ill. His teeth fell out, then his jaw and chin disintegrated. Half his face was missing. Openings in his skull exposed his brain. He wrapped his head in bandages to hold it together.

Robert Winn, an attorney with the Federal Trade Commission, told *Time* magazine in 1932:

> A more gruesome experience in a more gorgeous setting would be hard to imagine. Young in years and mentally alert, he could hardly speak. His head was swathed in bandages. He had undergone two successive operations in which his whole upper jaw, excepting two front teeth, and most of his lower jaw, had been removed. All the remaining bone tissue of his body was slowly disintegrating, and holes were actually forming in his skull.

Eben Byers.

Eben Byers died on April 2, 1932. He was buried in a lead-lined coffin in the family mausoleum in Pittsburgh. *The Wall Street Journal* later ran a story with the headline, "The Radium Water Worked Fine Until His Jaw Came Off." The doctor who prescribed Radithor continued to deny the product was harmful.

The FTC shut down Bailey's factory. By then, more than 400,000 bottles of Radithor had been sold. Bailey was never held to account for his deeds. In fact, he later founded the Radium Institute in New York, selling a radioactive belt clip and a device to make radioactive water.

Eben Byers' body was exhumed for examination in 1965 and was still highly radioactive.

William Bailey died of bladder cancer in 1949. His body was exhumed twenty years later and was also found to be highly radioactive.

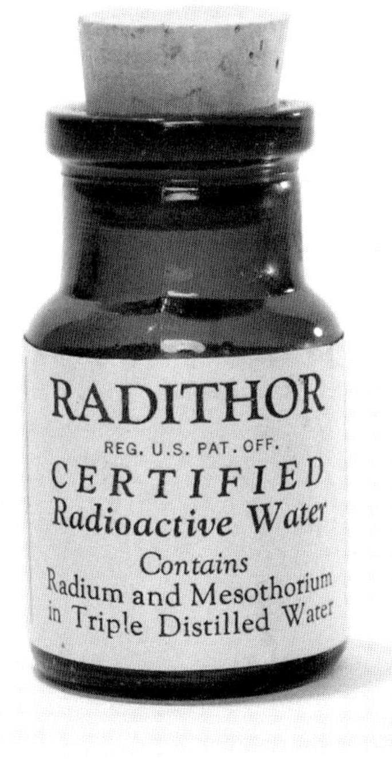

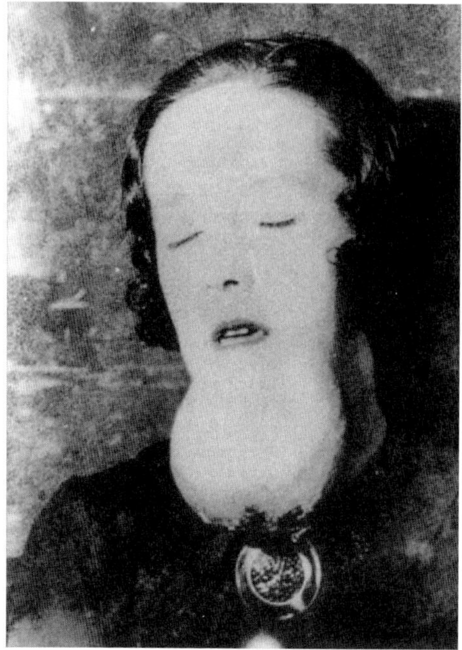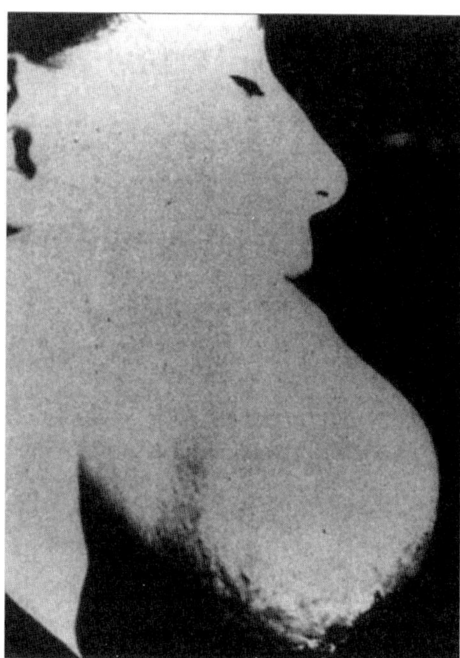

An example of "radium jaw."

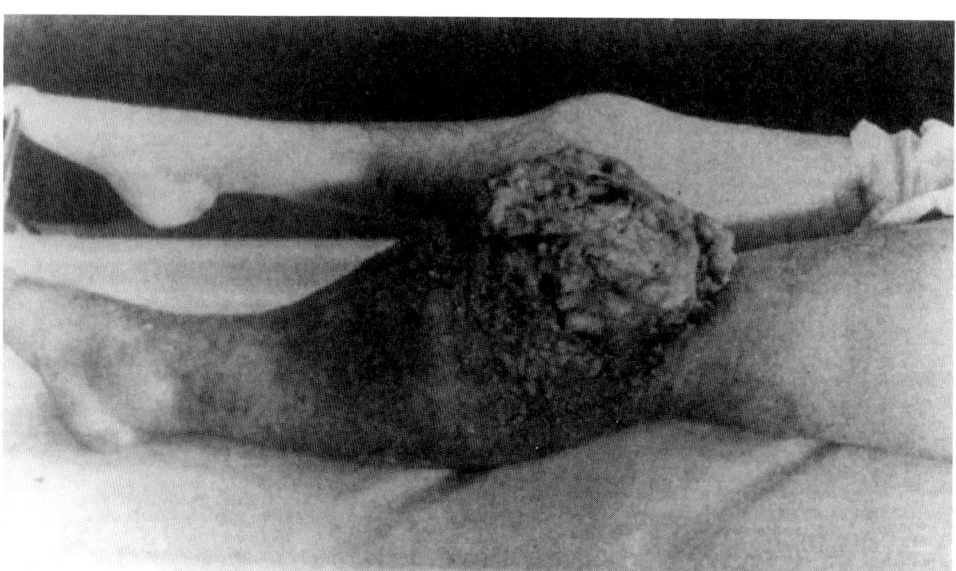

A cancerous tumor in the leg of a radium worker.

4

DEATH COMES TO OTTAWA

Dial painters were dying in New Jersey and Connecticut before anyone in Ottawa knew about the dangers from radium. The company managers in Ottawa knew about the dangers, yet they did not tell their workers.

By 1925, the managers in Ottawa knew their workers would read the newspapers about what was happening in New Jersey, so they tried to handle the situation. They had the workers take physical exams, with the goal of proving they were healthy. The tests did show radium in their bodies, but the company did not tell the women.

Radium Dial opened a second location in nearby Streator, in case the Ottawa women rebelled. The Streator location operated for nine months in 1925 (along with the Ottawa location) until the company was satisfied the Ottawa women would not quit.

When she was dying in 1938, Catherine Donohue told the *Chicago Times* about the process of painting the dials:

We worked with fine camel's hair brushes. In addition to painting the hands and numerals on luminous clocks and other instruments, there were such jobs as making luminous maps for airplane pilots and extra fine maps for astronomers.

It was fascinating work, and the pay was good. But it was exacting work, too. You can understand, every stroke of the brush, every line had to be just so. We didn't work with actual radium, of course. What we used was a preparation of radioactive salts, a by-product of radium. Later we learned that just to breathe in some of the dust from which the paint was made was deadly, but when I was there, one of the girls used to just sit at a table with a box of the dust in front of her and ladle it out.

Help wanted, 1922.

The radium paint was mixed in small saucers. Using a camel's hair brush, you have to have a fine point, and practically all the girls had the habit of wetting the brush with their tongues and lips. That's the way this terrible, terrible poison got into our systems. We never even knew it was harmful.

When I went to work in the Radium Dial plant, I had no idea of the terrible danger. In fact, I don't think the company itself knew the danger then.

The Radium Art Studio

Offers to young ladies of talent and character exceptional opportunities to learn an interesting and remunerative profession.

Call at 1022 Columbus Street, Ottawa
RADIUM DIAL COMPANY

The Radium Dial Art Studio, in the former high school building.

YOU ARE CORDIALLY INVITED

*By the Radium Art Studio of the Radium
Dial Company to Visit and Inspect
the Institution*

TOMORROW, APRIL 25

between the hours of 1:00 P. M. and 4:00 P. M.

They occupy what was previously the High School Building at 1022 Columbus Street, Ottawa. The Studios employ more than 100 artists. They handle the most expensive product in the world—radium.

Radium will be on display. The processes will be demonstrated.

Everybody in Ottawa and community welcome.

Saturday, April 25th, 1:00 P. M. to 4:00 P. M.

Radium Art Studio

of the

Radium Dial Company

1022 Columbus Street, Ottawa, Illinois

An invitation to visit the studio on April 25, 1925.

Radium Dial workers, 1926. Rufus Reed is seated in front in the white cap. Lottie Murray is behind him to the left, in a tie. Catherine Wolfe Donohue is in the black dress behind him to the left. Marguerite Glacinski is in the second row, just to the left of the man holding a white cap. Margaret Looney is behind Catherine Wolfe, just to the left, in a tie. Marie Becker Rossiter is the seventh person to the right of Miss Looney. Mary Duffy Robinson is the third person to the right of Mrs. Rossiter in the picture. Below is a close-up.

Mrs. Donohue worked at Radium Dial from 1922 to 1931. Lottie Murray, who was superintendent in 1922, taught the young women how to point the brushes with their tongues, Mrs. Donohue said.

Mercedes Reed, the wife of manager Rufus Reed, who also taught dial painting, would demonstrate to the women that the substance was not harmful by eating the radium paint off a spatula—or so the women thought.

The women wore their own clothes to work, not uniforms. They wore these clothes home at night and could see them glow in the dark. This radium was in addition to the radium they ingested as they put the tip of the brush to their mouths thousands of times, as well as the radium they absorbed by painting their eyelids, teeth, lips and buttons for the amusement of watching them glow in the dark.

One son of a dial painter told me the story of a woman who mixed the radium paint with water and drank it. She would urinate in the bathroom and amuse the other women by watching her pee glow in the dark.

It was in 1925 that the company told the women they could replace the brushes with glass pens. Some of the women still preferred the brushes because the pens were more difficult to use. The women were paid by how many dials they painted, and using a brush was faster.

Some of the Ottawa dial painters were becoming alarmed by the news of death in New Jersey. Two of the women, Catherine Donahue and Marie Rossiter, asked Mr. Reed why the company did not reveal the results of physical exams. He replied, "My dear girls, if we were to give a medical report to you girls, there would be a riot in the place."

The company placed a full-page advertisement in the *Ottawa Daily Republican-Times* on June 7, 1928, to calm fears. The advertisement said the paint in New Jersey, where the deaths occurred, contained mesothorium. The paint in Ottawa did not. Therefore, radium was safe and there was nothing to worry about.

Statement by the
Radium Dial Company:

In view of the wide circulation given reports of poisoning caused by paint used for luminous watch dials getting into the mouths of girls employed in applying it, it is time to call attention to an important fact that has as yet received only occasional mention in the news – namely, that though this condition is always called "radium" poisoning, we do not know of a case occurring in plants where radium alone has been used to make the paints.

So far as we have been able to learn, all the distressing cases of so called "radium" poisoning reported from the east, have occurred in establishments that have used luminous paint made altogether or in part from another radioactive material, called mesothorium.

Though mesothorium was cheaper than radium, the Radium Dial Company, because of its affiliation with the Standard Chemical Company, the largest producer of radium in the world, used for its work the material manufactured by that company, which contained pure radium only.

Dr. Frederick L. Hoffman, statistical expert of the Prudential Life Insurance Co. in speaking of the "radium" poisoning cases in the east, has said in the Journal of the American Medical Association (Vol. 85, No. 13) "The probable explanation for the non-occurrence of such cases at other plants is that mesothorium has not been used." There is other data on record against mesothorium, and a strong case exists against it. But very little has been published in the newspapers at any time about mesothorium, and consequently few people know or care much about it. Radium on the contrary, has been widely advertised, and therefore is being blamed, for a condition which better knowledge of the facts indicates radium has not caused, while those who produce the highly useful articles on which it is applied are unnecessarily worried and inconvenienced.

The Radium Dial Company has or has had, establishments in Ottawa, New York, Pittsburgh, Chicago, Streator and Peru. It has employed during a period of eleven years, over a thousand girls (many of whom have been with us for several years) and has produced many millions of luminous dials. We have at frequent intervals had thorough physical and medical examinations made by well known physicians and technical experts familiar with the conditions and symptoms of the so called "radium" poisoning. Nothing even approaching such symptoms or conditions has ever been found by these men. On the contrary, they have commented on the high standard of health and appearance of our employees, and the excellent conditions under which they work. If their reports had been unfavorable, or if we at any time had reason to believe that any conditions of the work endangered the health of our employees, we would at once have suspended operations.

The health of the employees of the Radium Dial Company is always foremost in the minds of its officials.

R. G. FORDYCE   JOSEPH A. KELLY
VICE-PRESIDENT   PRESIDENT

D. M. GOETSCHIUS
MANAGER

Ottawa Daily Republican-Times, June 7, 1928.

"The health of the employees of the Radium Dial Company is always foremost in the minds of its officials," the advertisement concluded.

The *Chicago Times* in 1938 cited a U.S. Labor Department statistic that one-thousandth of a milligram of this radioactive salt was enough to poison a human being—an amount that was too small to be seen by the most powerful microscope:

> Once lodged in the system, the salts send out emanations, "rays," that seemingly center their destructive forces upon the marrow of the bones and the white corpuscles of the blood. The result is bone decay and a sort of virulent anemia. There is no way known to medical science to combat the disease. Death is sure, agonizingly slow, the disease itself is horrible in its last stages.

The *Chicago Times* story added:

> A year ago, they were the doomed women of Ottawa. Today, they are the forgotten women. The hearing before the industrial commission this month will be their last stand—their last hope of collecting damages. And even here, the law will operate against them.

Radium Dial workers in Ottawa. Number 5 is Norma Payne. Number 11 is Catherine Payne. Number 12 is Ella Cruse.

Radium Dial was in the former Ottawa Township High School building.

Radium Dial workers in Ottawa.

They shoot to kill when it comes to cattle thieves in Illinois, and fish and fowl are safeguarded by stringent game laws—but womenfolk come cheap.

Chicago Times reporter Mary Doty wrote that great line in a March 17, 1936 story, as part of a series on the Ottawa victims. It was the first major publicity for the Ottawa radium victims, and it caused a sensation. Miss Doty wrote:

Chicago newspaper headlines told the story in 1936.

> If it were not so, there would be no story to tell of 600 young women who over a period of 10 to 15 years were subjected to the effect of a dangerous radioactive substance at the Radium Dial Co. of Ottawa ... There would be no horror tales of the dead and the dying that one hears at every hand in this small city of many churches.

Miss Doty cited ten deaths and fifteen who were dying. "Young girls who went blithely to work at the Dial a few short years ago now lie in several Ottawa cemeteries 'officially' dead from cancer, tumor, pneumonia, hemorrhage and other ailments," Miss Doty continued. "Others, still young, many of them mothers, hobble about their homes with locked hips, swollen limbs, their frames wracked with pain, an amputated arm, distorted faces."

She quoted the sister of one of the dead women, "It seems as if any of the girls who ever get anything the matter with them never get up again." Miss Doty began the next day's installment:

> Graveyards are for the old and tired—not for the young and life-loving. But in Ottawa graveyards, pleasant enough places, there are too many young girls and mothers, victims of radium poisoning—the human discards of one of the city's industries.

She continued, "Of course, the dead tell no tales. But some of the old folks, widowed husbands and children, still live to ponder why it must be so." Miss Doty's prose continued in her March 19 story:

> You meet them on the street, the doomed women of Ottawa; those nearest to death resigned; the slightly affected with a haunting fear in their eyes. Some creep along, unable to move beyond a snail's pace; another with an empty coat sleeve or a mutilated nose, withered hands, a shrunken jaw. Long after they are dead, scientists say, their bones will vibrate with the death-dealing alpha rays bombarding their skeletons at a speed of 18,000 miles a second. This is the price of the luminous clock faces, maps and dashboard gadgets.

Jeanette Byers had most of the bones in her nose removed before dying. Christina Halm lost her teeth and her jaw was so shrunken that she could not be fit for a set of false teeth. Norma DeGroot lost her teeth, and her legs were in constant pain. Norma's sister, Catherine Balda, also lost all her teeth. A sister-in-law, Pearl Payne, had nine operations already. Nellie Jacobs Holtrum had a tooth extracted and her gums bled for a month.

The *Chicago Times* listed several other victims: Ruth Thomson, Della Harbiston, Elsie Bry O'Shea, Gertrude Leroy, Frances O'Connell, Marguerite Glacinski, Irene Politte, Helen Munch, and Margaret Begwin.

5

LAWSUITS AGAINST RADIUM DIAL

Mary Ellen "Ella" Cruse was the first Ottawa dial painter to die, on September 4, 1927, at the age of twenty-four. Her family filed a lawsuit in July 1928, asking for $3,750 in damages. A hearing was set for February 26, 1929 in the courthouse in Ottawa. Swen Kjaer, an investigator for the U.S. Bureau of Labor Statistics, showed up, but he found it was postponed by Cruse's lawyer because he said he did not know enough about radium poisoning. The case later was settled for $250.

The Ottawa women had a hard time in their fight for compensation. No Ottawa doctor would certify radium poisoning as a cause of death, and no Ottawa lawyer would represent them. The general attitude of the city was that these women were giving Ottawa a bad name and making questionable claims against a big local employer.

Jay S. Cook, a Chicago lawyer, sued Radium Dial in July 1934 on behalf of Inez Vallat, Charlotte Purcell, and Marguerite Glacinski, asking $50,000 for each woman. The lawsuit relied on the state laws regarding workmen's compensation and occupational diseases.

It was an earlier Illinois tragedy that led to one of the nation's first workmen's compensation and occupational disease laws in 1911. The legislation came from the disaster in nearby Cherry in 1909, where 259 men and boys died in a coal mine fire. The Cherry tragedy also led to the creation of the Illinois Industrial Commission in 1917. The hearing on behalf of Catherine Donohue in 1938 was held before this commission.

Mrs. Vallat's lawsuit claimed that Radium Dial violated the Occupational Disease Act of 1911 by "carelessly and negligently" permitting the air in the factory "to be saturated with dust containing radium," which caused her illness. Radium Dial's lawyers countered that Mrs. Vallat was not an employee when she became ill and she did not file the lawsuit within the required two years after leaving work.

Mr. Cook took the case all the way to the Illinois Supreme Court, and he lost. The Illinois Supreme Court ruled in July 1935 that the Occupational Disease Act was unconstitutional because it was vague and "gave legislative powers to an administrative department of the state." Justice Paul Farthing delivered the verdict, writing that Mrs. Vallat had an "alleged illness" when he probably meant to say she claimed it allegedly was caused by her work.

Mr. Cook also represented Christine Halm, Olive West Witte, Catherine Wolfe Donohue, and Norma Payne DeGroot. Radium Dial's lawyer was Andrew J. O'Conor III of Ottawa. Mr. O'Conor also represented Libbey-Owens-Ford glass factory of Ottawa in nearly thirty-six cases brought by people claiming occupational disease.

The Vallat case was a landmark in dismissing worker's claims. Governor Henry Horner signed a new Occupational Disease Act in March 1936, which set a statute of limitations that did not help the radium victims, since some cancers from radium poisoning do not show up for fifteen or more years after exposure. The new law also covered silicosis, a problem that decades later would be a major issue (along with mesothelioma) at the Libbey-Owens-Ford factory in Ottawa.

Mr. Cook withdrew from the case on July 9, 1937, leaving the women without any legal representation less than two weeks before a hearing before the Illinois Industrial Commission. They could not find any other lawyer to represent them because they did not have the money to hire one.

Even if the women had won their case, the most they could win was about $667 each. That figure would be divided from the $10,000 bond that Radium Dial forfeited when they skipped town in 1937 to avoid such liability claims. The $10,000 workmen's compensation bond was required by Illinois law because Radium Dial had no insurance. Its policy was cancelled in 1928 because of the radium poisoning deaths, and it could find no other company to provide coverage.

Mr. Cook told the *Chicago Times*:

Please try to understand my position in withdrawing from the case. I hated to have to do it, but I simply couldn't afford to keep on.

Frankly, I've got to earn a living. When I took the case, the company was still doing business in Ottawa. Naturally, radium is no inexpensive stuff. Indeed, it's probably the most expensive substance in the world. We figured if we sued and won, there'd be plenty assets we could levy on. On that basis, I could afford to take the case, even though I had to advance all of the expenses. I never received anything from any of these women. I never asked for anything. I wouldn't have the heart to take it from them.

"The same applies now, only more so," Mr. Cook said. He cited the $667 figure, adding, "I'd look fine, chiseling in for a piece of that, wouldn't I?" He continued:

The Radium Dial Company has closed its plant it Ottawa and has skipped out from under, it is true. What they've done was they've abandoned the old company and formed a new corporation. That way, you see, the "new" corporation can't be held liable for anything the "old" company did.

The *Chicago Times* story added, "Without a lawyer, the women fear legal trickery. Indeed, so hopeless is their outlook that many of them may stay away."

Chicago Times writer John Main was outraged: "[The upcoming hearing] will be the next to the last act of what lawyers say is the biggest and most pitiful miscarriage of justice in the history of Illinois. The last act will be these women's deaths—sure, tortured, horrible—death that bears a close outward resemblance to leprosy or to a terrible cancer – death from radium poisoning."

The help of Clarence Darrow of Chicago was sought. Darrow was the most famous defense lawyer in the nation. Darrow was best known for the Scopes "Monkey Trial" evolution case and

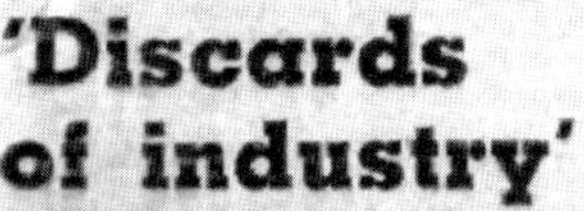

Mary Doty wrote breakthrough stories about the Ottawa radium victims for the *Chicago Times.*

the defense of "Thrill Killers" Nathan Leopold and Richard Loeb. Darrow was an idealistic lawyer known for taking cases based on principle rather than on a big fee.

Hobart Payne, whose wife, Pearl, was one of the former dial painters poisoned by radium, wrote to Darrow on May 17, 1937:

Dear Sir, It is as a last resort that I turn to you for assistance or advice. I do not know whether or not you are aware of the fact that or not but there exists in this county a group of young women whose life is gradually ebbing away from radium poisoning. Already nine have passed away to the great beyond and the tenth is fast approaching the grave. This condition is due to their employment at the Radium Dial Co. at Ottawa, Ill., one of the many DuPont-allied industries.

Due to the fact that radium poisoning does not become evident for a number of years after the inception of the poison, these girls have received no compensation for their injury.

They have turned to every legal agent and government department known to them without avail. Social complications are involved because due to their activity, business interests, politicians and the clergy have been robbed of the income derived from the wages of former employees. This company has been moved to N.Y.

Mr. Thomas Donohue of Ottawa, who has vigorously opposed the operation of this plant in the above city, has been persecuted, and the controlling interests have even tried to bring a charge of insanity against him. This man is also writing to you in a frantic effort to receive some advice or assistance. His wife is in a pitiable condition (on) account of this poisoning. Part of her jaw bone has recently broke through the flesh and came out into her mouth.

These cases are to come before the industrial commission for a final hearing on May 25, 1937. And there (is) no attorney to represent these girls. Would it be possible for you to take up this case and do what you can for these women? I am positive this case would be won with your assistance or legal advice. If it is not possible for you to do so, could you refer this case to a good reputable social minded attorney whom you think would handle this?

Hoping to hear from you soon. I remain, Hobart J. Payne, 605 Todd Street, LaSalle.

Darrow replied that he was too old to take the case (he would die on March 13, 1938, a month short of his eighty-first birthday). However, he recommended another Chicago lawyer who also fought for justice. So, when everything looked hopeless for the Ottawa victims, a hero stepped in to help them.

Leonard J. Grossman told the court he would represent the Ottawa women at the upcoming hearing. Mr. Grossman, a former assistant corporation counsel for the city of Chicago, met with five of the women—Marie Rossiter, Margaret Glacinski, Frances O'Connell, Catherine Donohue, and Pearl Payne—in his office at 134 N. LaSalle Street in Chicago, in July 1937.

"New hope for Ottawa's doomed women, victims of radium poisoning, appeared today as the Illinois Industrial Commission met here for consideration of their cases," is how the *Chicago Times* led their story on July 23.

A hearing was set for February 1938 before the Illinois Industrial Commission. Mr. Grossman represented fourteen women, but this hearing focused on the case of just one victim, Catherine Donohue. Catherine Donohue worked at Radium Dial for nine years. She started when the company opened, when she was nineteen years old. For six years, she worked next to Inez Vallat.

Former Radium Dial workers went to Leonard Grossman's Chicago law office in July 1937 to have him represent them before the Illinois Industrial Commission. From left are Marie Rossiter, Marguerite Glacinski, Frances O'Connell, Catherine Donohue, and Pearl Payne. Mr. Grossman's secretary, Carol Reiser, is seated.

6

THE DONOHUE HEARING
OF 1938

Two days of hearings were scheduled for February 10 and 11, 1938 at the LaSalle County courthouse in downtown Ottawa. Catherine Donohue's case was the first one to be heard. Catherine Donohue testified that she was fired by Radium Dial by assistant manager Rufus Reed in 1931 when her limping became "noticeable" to other workers. She said Reed told her that her condition "was embarrassing to the company."

"Your limping condition is causing talk. We'll have to let you go," Reed told her. Company President Joseph Kelly and Vice President Rufus Fordyce were there when Reed said this. She went on to testify:

> Even now, my body gives off a faint luminous glow when surrounded by darkness ... In my dark bathroom at night, my hands, hair and clothes would shine from rubbing the radium preparation on them at work.
>
> My clothes, hanging in a dark closet, gave off a phosphorescent glare. When I walked along the street, I was aglow from the radium powder. We even ate our lunches on the work tables near the luminous paint and brushes which we used.

Mr. Grossman introduced as evidence an advertisement from June 7, 1928, in the *Ottawa Daily Republican Times* by Radium Dial, just after the New Jersey radium scare. The full-page advertisement had been posted on the company bulletin board in 1928. Mrs. Donohue cited that advertisement, saying her bosses used it to assure the women their paint was not harmful. She described the method used. "We used Japanese art brushes. We would first dip them into water, then into the (radium) powder and then point the ends of the bristles between our lips."

The only warning in the lunchroom, she said, was to not get any food on the dials. When asked by Mr. Grossman, Mrs. Donohue said the bosses did not instruct the women to wash their hands before eating lunch.

Mrs. Donohue said the company eventually provided glass pens in place of brushes, but they did not tell the women that the United States government condemned the use of camel's hair brushes in radium painting, and there were no notices posted about the dangers of using brushes. The women were given the choice of a brush or a glass pen, she said, but the glass pens were very clumsy to handle.

She said she began to have fainting spells, and then a pain in her left ankle which spread to her hip. "My hip joints locked and I could hardly walk." Mrs. Donohue testified that she was told by a doctor in 1934 that she had radium poisoning. She said when she told Rufus Reed, he replied, "There is nothing to it, we don't have radium poisoning at all."

Mrs. Donohue said that other women at the plant were given medical examinations. "At no time (the company) warned the employees of any danger in using the compound," she said.

Catherine Donohue and Marie Rossiter testified that they asked Reed why he would not post the results of their medical exams. They repeated his incredible reply that he did not tell them because he feared they would start a riot.

Mrs. Donohue said she and Mrs. Rossiter did not realize what he meant because the truth of what radium could do was kept from them at the time. Marie Rossiter worked at Radium Dial for seven years, beginning in 1923. She quit when her son, William, was born. The bones in Mrs. Donohue's face crumbled from the effects of the radium. She lost her teeth, her jawbone and other bones disintegrated, and she had difficulty speaking. Mrs. Donohue opened a small jewelry box in the court room and took out two pieces of her jawbone.

Chicago Herald and Examiner reporter Bruce Grant wrote, "Mrs. Donohue seemed like one already dead. She was covered to the chin with a bed spread and her head was propped up on pillows. She kept her eyes closed and her mouth slightly open."

The LaSalle County courthouse in downtown Ottawa, in the 1950s.

Arthur Magid, lawyer for Radium Dial, and Leonard Grossman, lawyer for the dial painters, with Thomas Donohue and Charlotte Purcell.

"Her emaciated body shaking, Mrs. Donohue was a pathetic witness," wrote *Chicago Times* reporter Helen McKenna. "Her fingers twisted a scapular medal as she told of not being able to attend Catholic church services. Her crumbling hip bone will not permit her to kneel, she testified. A priest now brings communion to her at home."

After Mrs. Donohue finished, Dr. Walter Dalitsch testified that Mrs. Donohue's condition was poisoning by radioactive material. Mr. Grossman asked him if Mrs. Donohue's condition was temporary or permanent. It was permanent, the doctor replied. "Is it fatal?" Mr. Grossman asked.

"Now, er, I would prefer not to state in presence of the witness," the doctor said. The doctor looked at Mrs. Donohue and she collapsed. She could see it in his eyes. She was carried out of the court room. Dr. Dalitsch continued. "In my opinion, her death is almost certain within a matter of months. With certain treatment, she might live several years, but she cannot live for long."

Bruce Grant wrote:

Mrs. Donohue sobbed, slipped down in her chair and covered her face. Grossman and Dr. Sidney Weiner, a witness, aided by her husband Thomas, picked up the chair in which she was huddled and carried it from the room. The woman's sobs could be heard from the corridor.

Several other women, survivors of the group of one-time employees of the radium company, paled and shuddered. Nine of their friends and former fellow workers already were dead.

Mrs. Donohue was carried to the county clerk's office and laid on a desk, with birth records as a pillow. She clutched her husband's hand. "Don't leave me, Tom! Stay with me always!" The newspaper said she was too weak for tears.

Dr. Dalitsch continued. He said Mrs. Donohue's illness was fatal, and she was afflicted with osteonecrosis resulting from "radio-activated" poisoning in her jawbone.

Dr. Charles Loffler, a blood specialist from Chicago, testified that he diagnosed her with radium poisoning in 1934. He said alpha rays caused the red blood cells to shrink. "I don't give her long to live. She is doomed."

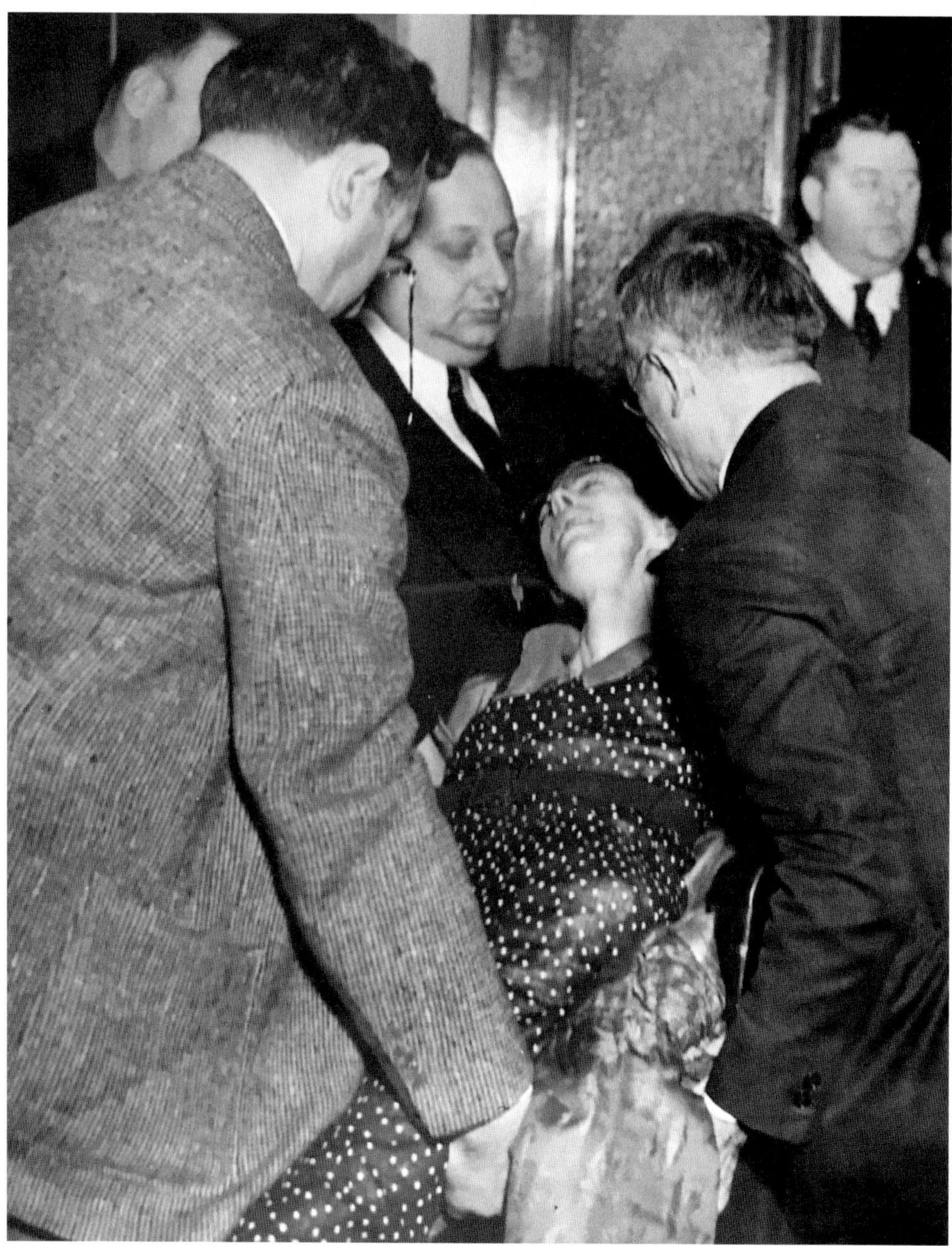

Catherine Donohue collapsed in the LaSalle County courthouse in Ottawa on February 10, 1938, after hearing testimony from Dr. Dalitsch that she would soon die. Her husband, Tom, is on the right assisting her.

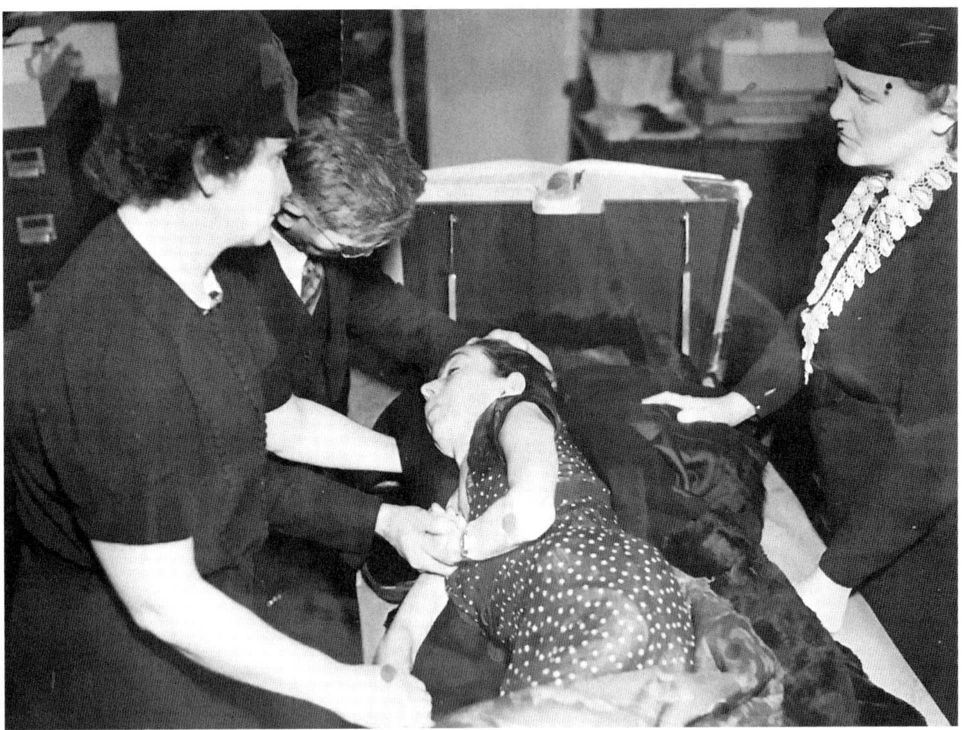

Pearl Payne and Thomas Donohue comfort Catherine Donohue after her collapse in the courthouse.

Thomas Donohue returned to the courthouse, after having taken his wife home. He wept when he heard this testimony.

Arthur Magid, Radium Dial's lawyer, objected to the testimony of the doctors who said Mrs. Donohue had a short time to live, saying it was "immaterial." Mr. Magid argued Mrs. Donohue's condition was not caused by poison, saying radium was abrasive but not a poison. Mr. Magid said the paint formula was five to ten parts of radium to a million parts of zinc, with iron sulphide and traces of copper. Mr. Grossman replied that, for the record, the company's 1928 advertisement stated that pure radium was used. Mr. Magid presented no evidence, only the argument that radium was not a poison. Even if radioactive elements did penetrate her, he argued, it is not a poison.

Eight other workers were there to testify: Charlotte Purcell, Marie Rossiter, Olive Witt, Marguerite Glacinski, Pearl Payne, Frances O'Connell, Maxine Smith, and Helen Munch.

Marie Rossiter, a thirty-two-year-old mother of one child, testified that Rufus Reed told her there was no danger with the radium paint. "Mr. Reed said we didn't have anything to worry about. He said radium would put rosy cheeks on us, that it was good for us." This was after the scare about the New Jersey women became public.

Miss Glacinski, who painted dials from 1924 to 1931, agreed, saying Mr. Reed told her that "the radium paint would make you girls good looking."

Charlotte Purcell told an Ottawa reporter that her left arm was amputated after a tumor started spreading toward her heart. Pearl Payne testified said she almost died from her illnesses and was now sterile.

Pearl Payne, Frances O'Connell, Marguerite Glacinski, Helen Munch, and Marie Rossiter at the 1938 hearing.

Helen Munch, Marie Rossiter, Marguerite Glacinski, Olive Witt, Frances O'Connell, and Maxine Smith, at the 1938 hearing.

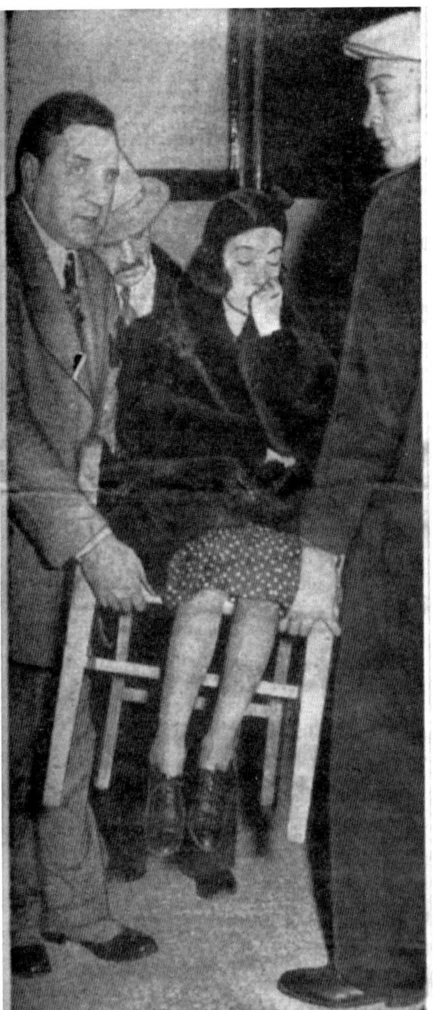

Mrs. Catherine Donohue, radium poisoning victim, being carried from Ottawa, Ill., courtroom after collapsing as doctor sealed her doom. Carrying her are Attorney Leonard J. Grossman of Chicago (left), and Clarence Witt, husband of another victim of the dread malady. Bending solicitiously over Mrs. Donohue is her husband, Thomas. (Evening American photo.)

Victim Faints at Death Query in Radium Suit

By HELEN McKENNA
(TIMES Staff Correspondent)

Ottawa, Ill., Feb. 10.—After identifying two pieces of her jawbone allegedly eaten away by radium poisoning, Mrs. Catherine Donohue collapsed today when her attorney asked a doctor if the disease was fatal.

Mrs. Donohue, one of Ottawa's "living dead," did not hear Dr. Walter M. Dalitsch, 30 N. Michigan ave., Chicago, answer she was doomed to die.

She was carried to the county clerk's office and stretched on a desk with birth records as a pillow.

"Don't leave me, Tom—stay with me always," she said clutching her husband's hand.

Too weak for tears, Mrs. Donohue was taken home to prepare for another ordeal as a witness tomorrow.

Dr. Dalitsch, a former dentist and now a surgeon, testified Mrs. Donohue was afflicted with osteonecrosis resulting from "radio-activated" poisoning in her jawbone.

He said there was "a direct cause and relation" between her condition and her former employment. Mrs. Donohue testified she worked for the Radium Dial Co. from 1922 to 1931.

BONE PIECES SHOWN

In muffled, faltering tones, the frail mother, who weighs 71 pounds, testified before Arbitrator George Marvell of the Illinois Industrial commission. She said her entire jaw is crumbling.

Six other women victims whose last hope of justice lies with the commission shuddered when pieces of bone were introduced. Their fate may be the same as Mrs. Donohue's.

Atty. Leonard J. Grossman, for Mrs. Donohue, and Walter Bachrach, for the Radium Dial Co., have agreed her compensation battle will be a test case.

"In my dark bathroom at night," Mrs. Donohue testified, "my hands, hair and clothes would shine from rubbing the radium preparation on them at work."

Despite company objection, Grossman introduced as evidence advertisement signed by company officials which appeared in the Ottawa Daily Republican Times June 7, 1928, that, after a New Jersey radium scandal, told workers not to worry, radium painting would not harm them.

Mrs. Donohue stopped to gulp water before testifying the advertisement was posted on company bulletin boards.

Radium Dial Co., which allegedly skipped Ottawa last year leaving nine women employes dead and 15 others doomed to hideous deaths, moved to New York, where it is still operating. A $10,000 bond was posted with the industrial commission. Atty. Grossman, however, contends it is now but $5,000.

OLD LAW SCRAPPED

When the "suicide club" began its battle for recompense, Illinois law deprived doomed women of standing in court. The old ... within six months after contraction of disease.

Radium poisoning takes three or more years to develop to a point where even an expert diagnostician can recognize symptoms.

The antiquated law was scrapped when the State Supreme court declared it unconstitutional and a new law clarifying rates of compensation for victims of occupational diseases was signed by Gov. Horner, March 16, 1936.

CAN'T ATTEND CHURCH

Her emaciated body shaking, Mrs. Donohue was a pathetic witness. Her fingers twisted a scapular medal as she told of not being able to attend Catholic church services. Her crumbling hip bone will not permit her to kneel, she testified. A priest now brings communion to her at home.

Dr. Charles Loffler, 22 W. Randolph st., said he treated Mrs. Donohue in 1934 and after X-ray and dental examinations, diagnosed her illness as radium poisoning.

When the radium company opened in New York as a "new" corporation, it escaped liability for damages asked by the doomed women. Amount of its posted bond is all the women can hope to recover unless old assets can be traced to the new company.

This, Atty. Grossman claims, can be done.

TELLS PLANT METHODS

Mrs. Donohue, her rendezvous with death nearing, explains methods used in the plant: "We worked with fine, camel hair brushes. We didn't work with actual radium, of course. What we used was a preparation of radioactive salts, a by-product of radium. Using a camel's hair brush you have to have a fine point and practically all the girls had the habit of wetting the brush with their tongues and lips."

"That's the way this terrible poison got into our systems. We ..."

... day's fight for compensation to ease days before inevitable death. They are Mrs. Charlotte Purcell, 6720 S. Halsted st. and Miss Helen Munch, 3423 N. Avers ave. Other victims at the hearing were Marguerite Glacinski, Pearl Payne, Marie Rossiter and Mrs. Olive West Witt.

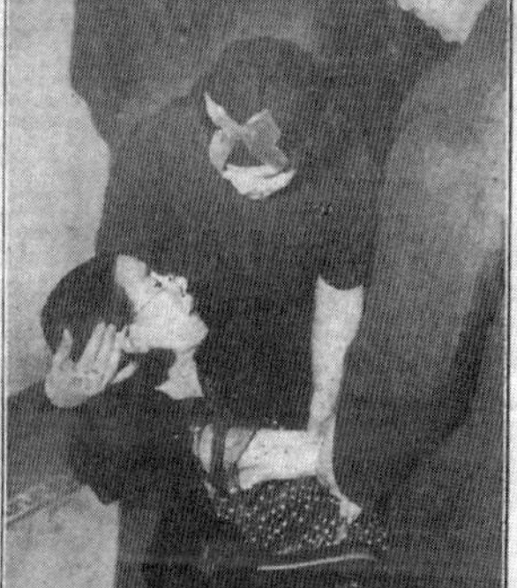

COLLAPSE!—Screaming in hysteria, radium poisoned Mrs. Catherine Donohue faints at Ottawa hearing today. (Exclusive TIMES photo (c) 1938).

Mrs. Charlotte Purcell

Helen Munch

The second day of the hearing was in the Donohue house. Mr. Grossman is next to Mrs. Donohue. Charlotte Purcell, Pearl Payne, and Frances O'Connell are behind her.

The hearings continued the next day in the Donohue home at 520 E. Superior Street because Catherine was too weak to get off of her couch. She slept through part of the testimony.

A number of other women testified. Mrs. Purcell said Rufus Reed told her radium "would put rosy cheeks on us, that it was good for us." Pearl Payne, Helen Munch, Olive Witt, Margaret Glacinski, and Frances O'Connell gave similar testimonies. Margaret and Frances were sisters.

Mrs. Donohue told her story at the hearing, even though the great strain threatened her life. "It's too late for me, but maybe it will help some of the others," she told the *Chicago Times*.

Helen McKenna interviewed Mrs. Donohue from her bed after the hearing:

What slim thread binds her to life, a thread medical experts say must snap at any moment. Mrs. Donohue responded, "I will live. It's the fighting Irish."

Suddenly, I forgot her crumbled teeth, the shattered jaws that muffled a cultured voice. I forgot the tragic remnants that radium poisoning left of a once handsome woman. I saw briefly the soul that holds her husband's love—love grown blind to the fragile shell of a woman that is all other people see.

Mrs. Donohue told her, "People are afraid to talk to me now. Sometimes it makes me terribly lonesome. They act as though I'm already a corpse. It's hard to have so many people around and still be so alone."

Even her former co-workers avoid her, Miss McKenna wrote, possibly because they see her "as a warning of their own doom."

DOOMED TO TORTURED, HORRIBLE DEATH!—Marked for death from "radium poisoning" contracted while an employe of Radium Dial Co. of Ottawa, Ill., Mrs. Charlotte Purcell, 31, 6749 S. Halsted st., lives in daily fear of end that is inevitable. Yet, her last chance of collecting damages along with 14 other doomed women workers—at hearing before Illinois industrial commission July 25 at Ottawa—may bring only $667.   (Story on page 3)

Olive Witt, Frances O'Connell, and Maxine Smith.

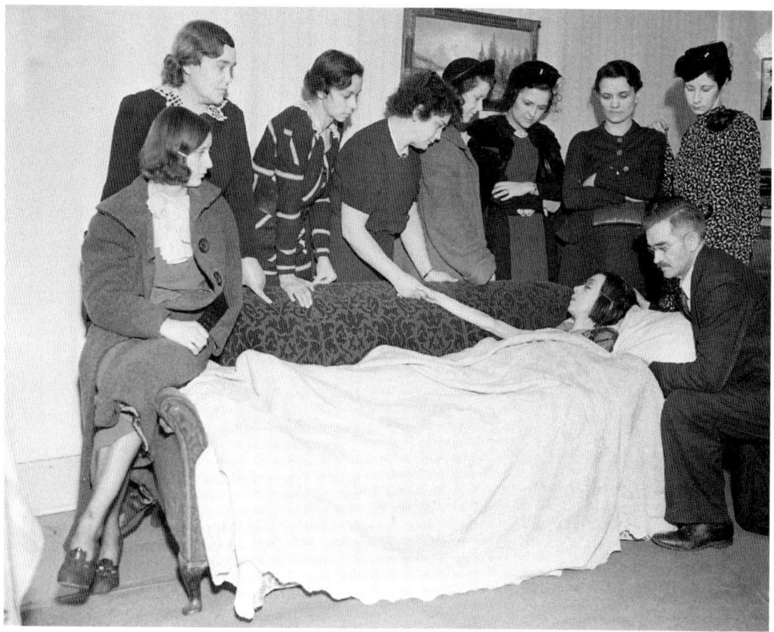

Catherine Donohue had to have the hearing on February 11, 1938, in her home because she was confined to the couch. Her husband, Thomas, is beside her. Other victims, from left, are Charlotte Purcell, Olive Witt, Marie Rossiter, Pearl Payne, Frances O'Connell, Marguerite Glacinski, Maxine Smith, and Helen Munch.

Nine Facing Death With Smile; Their Courage a Sermon of Hope

Last Wishes Told
Doomed Women Meet

Radium Victims Seek to Aid Children— Before They Die

Through their pain and the dread of being taken by death from their loved ones, nine young women suffering from radium poisoning had the courage to hope and smile Sunday.

They prayed, too; prayed that from the world's medical laboratories might come a reprieve from their apparent sentence to death. In a modest little home in Ottawa, Ill., their very calmness and courage preached a sermon of hope.

WANT TO SAVE OTHERS.

There was no horror among them of death itself. Each declared that, if the fates decree, she will face the next world with the realization that her sacrifice may have saved others.

Eight of them stood today at the bedside of the ninth, Mrs. Catherine Wolfe Donohue, whose condition is the most serious. The eight, who can still walk, though some with great difficulty, were called together by Attorney Leonard J. Grossman for what may be their farewell to Mrs. Donohue.

PLEA STUDIED.

The wraith-like woman, mother of two children, collapsed last week during a hearing before Arbitrator George B. Marvel of the Illinois Industrial Commission. Her plea for compensation

Gathered about Mrs. Catherine Donohue are the eight other victims of radium poisoning. From the left they are Mrs. Charlotte Purcell, Mrs. Olive Witt, Mrs. Marie Rossiter, Mrs. Pearl Payne, Mrs. Frances O'Connell, Miss Margaret Glacinski, Mrs. Maxxine Smith and Miss Helen Munch. Sitting beside Mrs. Donohue is her husband, Thomas.

Chicago Herald and Examiner, February 14, 1938.

Several of the women who testified at the hearing gave statement to the *Chicago Herald and Examiner* reporter, including what they would do if they won any money in their claim. Charlotte Purcell said, "I would use the money for medicine and for insurance for my husband and the children. I will spend my last months in the company of my children."

Pearl Payne said, "I am missing so much of life now—the chance of being a mother again, the chance of being the wife my fine husband deserves. I regret that I have not been able to give my daughter an education."

Marie Rossiter said, "I have read all the literature on my disease and I know too much to expect recovery, but I am still hoping for it. I want to see everything I possibly can and show my seven-year-old boy and my husband the bravest smile I can until the end."

Maxine Smith said, "I am more concerned about how my three girls will get along when the end comes. I am afraid that the radium may have been passed on to them and they may have the same fate."

Olive Witt and Frances O'Connell regretted not being able to play with their children and said their money would go to medical bills and to their children.

Helen Munch said, "I would want to be in a hospital and away from everybody so that they would only remember me when I had good health."

Margaret Glacinski said, "I will spend my last few months getting everything out of life. But if the courts say that I am entitled to money, I would use it to organize a committee to educate radium sufferers and get the laws to protect them. I would take up their battle."

After the hearing, Leonard Grossman announced the formation of "The Society of the Living Dead." It was a term that others, particularly newspapers looking for sensation, had used. "The purpose of the society is to obtain better protection, by legislation and otherwise, for persons endangered by occupational diseases," Mr. Grossman said.

The idea came from Pearl Payne. The society was organized in late February 1938 in Mr. Grossman's office in Chicago, with Marie Rossiter, Pearl Payne, Charlotte Purcell, and Thomas Donohue.

In March 1938, Arthur Magid filed an argument with the Illinois Industrial Commission, claiming that a poison is absorbed into the blood, and since radium is not absorbed into the blood, it is not poisonous. Mr. Grossman replied that the dictionary defines as poison any substance that destroys the life or impairs the health of a person.

The decision came in April 1938 from George Marvel, the arbitrator for the Illinois Industrial Commission. He ruled that Radium Dial was responsible for Mrs. Donohue's illness, and he awarded her $3,470, and an annual pension of $277, which was to begin in June 1940. The $3,470 figure was based on $11 a week, from April 25, 1934 to June 1, 1940, at which time the lifetime pension was to begin. Mrs. Donohue gave a weak smile at the news and said, "I'll have to suffer more."

Fourteen other women were to get compensation, based on the length of their employment and the extent of their illness. Mr. Marvel said the disease was "slow and insidious" and "progressive and extending over a long period of years" and Mrs. Donohue had no knowledge of it until it was too late. Arthur Magid appealed that decision.

Mrs. Donohue said she would not live to see the money, but perhaps it would help her husband, who had been out of work for several months at the height of the Great Depression.

Meanwhile, the news from the New Jersey scandal continued to be told. In May 1938, Margaret Laudate, the thirty-eight-year-old mother of three, became the twenty-seventh woman who worked in Radium Dial's plant in Orange, New Jersey, to die of radium poisoning.

Herald Chicago and Examiner
SUNDAY—FEBRUARY 27—1938
TEN CENTS
GHOST WOMEN AWAIT COURT'S DECISION ON RADIUM POISONING
HEARING BRINGS OUT STORY OF FATAL METAL
'I Did This Thousands of Times'
OUTLOOK FOR U. S. TRADE IN 1938 IS BRIGHT
MRS. DONOHUE SHOWS HOW GIRLS USED DEADLY SOLUTION.
Questioning her in home at Ottawa is Attorney Leonard J. Grossman.

'LIVING DEATH' VICTIM WINS

Mrs. Donohue weighed 125 pounds when she went to work at the plant in 1922. She weighed just 70 pounds at the time of the hearings in February 1938. By the beginning of July, she would be down to 60 pounds. Catherine Donohue did not live to see a penny she had won. She died on July 27, 1938, in her home, at the age of thirty-five.

The next day, Mr. Grossman told the *Chicago Times* that Radium Dial needed to be investigated "so they could be made to pay for their sins." He called Mrs. Donohue's death "a cool, calculating money-making murder."

"Company officials knew the hazard," he told the *Chicago Times* reporter. "They should have warned Catherine and the other girls of the danger. But they didn't, and thus made themselves responsible for the awful consequences."

Radium Dial went to great lengths to fight every claim and judgment. They might have spent less on settlements than they did on lawyers, but they felt they had to discredit the women in order to avoid future lawsuits.

Radium Dial wanted the circuit court to take the jurisdiction from the Illinois Industrial Commission in the hope of having the court overturn the judgment. LaSalle County Circuit Clerk Edward Ryan refused to file the appeal until the company posted a $10,000 bond. Continental Casualty Insurance Company had dropped Radium Dial in November 1928. The insurance company told Radium Dial its work was on a prohibited list of Illinois insurance companies.

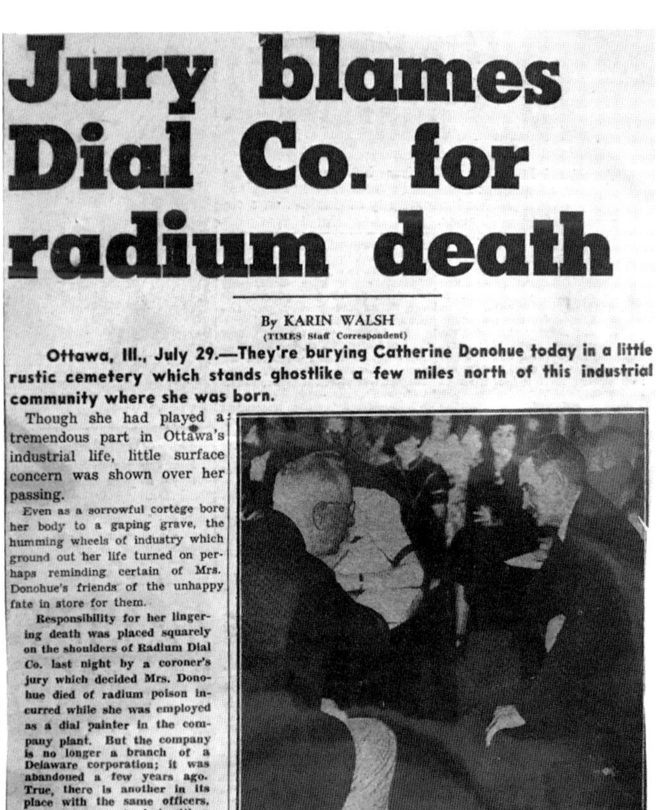

Jury blames Dial Co. for radium death

By KARIN WALSH
(TIMES Staff Correspondent)

Ottawa, Ill., July 29.—They're burying Catherine Donohue today in a little rustic cemetery which stands ghostlike a few miles north of this industrial community where she was born.

Though she had played a tremendous part in Ottawa's industrial life, little surface concern was shown over her passing.

Even as a sorrowful cortege bore her body to a gaping grave, the humming wheels of industry which ground out her life turned on perhaps reminding certain of Mrs. Donohue's friends of the unhappy fate in store for them.

Responsibility for her lingering death was placed squarely on the shoulders of Radium Dial Co. last night by a coroner's jury which decided Mrs. Donohue died of radium poison incurred while she was employed as a dial painter in the company plant. But the company is no longer a branch of a Delaware corporation; it was abandoned a few years ago. True, there is another in its place with the same officers, the same accounts, but with a different name and a different corporate identity.

Radium death inquest—Dr. H. S. Lester,

The fight went all the way to the Illinois Supreme Court, which ruled against the company in February 1939. Ottawa lawyer Andrew O'Conor and Arthur Magid represented Radium Dial in their losing effort.

Radium Dial would not pay anything to the Donohue estate. Radium Dial appealed the case on several points. In June 1939, the Illinois Supreme Court ruled against them. In October 1939, the United States Supreme Court again ruled against Radium Dial. It was the seventh time Mr. Grossman had won a decision for Mrs. Donohue and the dial painters.

7

RADIUM STORIES

Mary Ellen "Ella" Cruse was the first Ottawa dial painter to die, on September 4, 1927, at the age of twenty-four. Ella was the first Ottawa radium victim to be diagnosed.

Her cause of death was listed as "streptococcal septicemia infection of the face." Ella was the daughter of James and Nellie Cruse. He was a shipping clerk at the King & Hamilton farm machinery plant in Ottawa and they lived at 1119 Clinton Street. Ella Cruse is buried in St. Columba Cemetery, Ottawa. Nellie Cruse told the *Chicago Times*:

> I never wanted Ella to work there, more so after those New Jersey girls died. But it was a clean place and they were a jolly bunch of girls. She was there almost two years, but the last year she wasn't well, felt tired all the time and there was no life to her. A pimple appeared on the left side of her face about two weeks before she died.
>
> She came home Friday noon from work and the next day we went to the doctor. She told him how I was always afraid of her working at the Dial. He said, 'That's all bunk, there's not a cleaner place.' That was Saturday night, the week before she died. Tuesday, the doctor came to the house. He opened the pimple, nothing came out. She suffered the awfulest pain I ever saw anyone suffer. The next day he looked at her face and ordered her to the hospital. She died Sunday morning.

During the summer before Ella died, she had a hard ridge under her chin and had pain in her hands and legs. Mr. and Mrs. Cruse asked an Ottawa lawyer about compensation, and he told them to go to Chicago to look for a lawyer. The lawyer said it would cost $200 to exhume the body. The family did not have the money.

Inez Corcoran married Vincent Vallat on October 20, 1926. Two years later, she began suffering from the effects of radium poisoning after having worked at Radium Dial for six years. She was only twenty-three years old in 1929, but she was suffering from constant headaches, her teeth were falling out, and she needed a bandage to hold her jaw in place. She lost 20 pounds that year.

For the last five years of her life, Inez's hips were locked, and she could not move forward or backward. For the last three years of her life, one side of her face drained constantly.

Mary Ellen "Ella" Cruse.

Ottawa doctors could not help, so Inez went to the Mayo Clinic. They diagnosed radium poisoning; yet when she died in 1936 at the age of twenty-nine, the local doctors who signed her death certificate said her death was not related to her work. She is buried in Ottawa Avenue Cemetery.

Mary (Duffy) Robinson died on May 20, 1934, at the age of twenty-eight. She worked at Radium Dial for three years but spent seven years suffering before she died. Mary's mother told the *Chicago Times*:

> They cut off her right arm after it burst open. That was in January before she died. She never got out of bed again. The pain in her legs was terrible. They were all swollen out of shape. Sometimes when she was sitting down she'd have a terrible pain all of a sudden so that she would almost collapse.

Even though a sliver of Mary's arm was bone confirmed as radium poisoning by a New York laboratory, the Ottawa doctor who signed the death certificate listed "general sarcoma" as the cause and said her death was not related to her occupation.

Charlotte (Nevins) Purcell was born on January 27, 1906, in Ottawa, the youngest of six children of Patrick and Tillie Nevins of 1839 Columbus Street. She married Albert Purcell on April 12, 1928, in St. Columba Catholic Church. They had three children: Donald, Patricia, and Jean Ann.

Charlotte worked at Radium Dial for thirteen months, which was long enough to get a tumor that took her left arm. She began having swelling and pain in 1933. The doctors told her it was rheumatism and told her to use hot towels. However, that made it worse. The doctors then said it was tuberculosis, and then cancer. Charlotte finally saw a Chicago doctor, and he amputated her left arm at the shoulder just in time.

Charlotte Purcell demonstrates how painters put the brush to their lips. Her left arm was gone by then.

Mrs. Charlotte Purcell spends precious minutes—numbered by ravages of radium disease—with her three children (l. to r.)— Patsy, 6; Donald, 8; and Jean Ann, 5.

Catherine (Browne) Reavy died in 1946 at the age of thirty-nine. Her family said she glowed in the dark. She was one of the women later studied by Argonne National Laboratory, whose report said her body had "a considerable amount (of radium) and would have conferred on her a substantial risk of bone cancer."

Agnes, Sylvia, and Sadie Pray were sisters who all worked at Radium Dial. Sadie was born on September 28, 1905. She was twenty-six years old when she died on December 10, 1931. Sadie developed "a big black lump" on her forehead just after she died. There was no autopsy. The doctors said the cause of death was "pneumonia."

Sylvia (Pray) Nelson was born on August 9, 1903. She worked at Radium Dial for eight months in 1925. It was several years before symptoms developed, and she died a painful death from radium poisoning on August 2, 1955. She was fifty-two years old. Agnes (Pray) Pittman worked there for six months in 1924. Agnes also suffered for years with a variety of health problems before her death in 1982 at the age of seventy-four. The sisters are buried in Ottawa Avenue Cemetery.

Mildred (Bowers) Riskedahl of Marseilles worked at Radium Dial in the late 1920s. She developed a tumor in her stomach "the size of a blue ribbon watermelon," her grandson, Wayne Riskedahl, said. Fortunately, it was benign, and it was removed. She lived a long life before ending up with dementia in a nursing home. "She was such a sweet soul," Wayne said. "She was a glorious woman with a wicked sense of humor!"

Alma (Bagley) Whittaker worked at Radium Dial and Luminous Processes in the 1930s and 1940s. She worked in the office and handed out paint to the women. Still, she developed a rare form of cancer on her arm in 1980. She died two years later at the age of sixty-eight.

Other women went through miscarriages, extreme pain, and cancers, and Ottawa doctors refused to admit it was related to radium, even though they knew just what radium could do.

Mary (Vicini) Tonielli died on February 22, 1930 at the age of twenty-one. She was born in Italy and came here with her parents as an infant. She was just thirteen when she was hired in 1922, and she was not the youngest worker hired. She had been married less than two years when she died. Mary is buried in Ottawa Avenue Cemetery.

Mary Tonielli's sister, Anita Bernardini, also worked at Radium Dial, as did their sister-in-law Alma Travi. Alma had many health problems and later was part of a study by Argonne National Laboratory. Mike Kohr, a descendant in the family, said Anita and Alma shared a modest apartment. "When the light was turned out, they could see their fingertips, nose and lips glow in the dark," he said.

Marie (Becker) Rossiter was born on April 10, 1904. She grew up poor and went to work when she was thirteen. She married Patrick Rossiter and they had a son, William. Marie worked at Radium Dial for seven years. She left in 1930 to care for her son. Marie Rossiter had more determination and personality than ten people combined. Her granddaughter, Patty Gray, said Marie could do anything, from coming up with homemade cures for various ailments to entertaining her high school friends with stories.

It was a few years after leaving Radium Dial when Marie started having pain in her hip. She went to the "company hospital" on Ottawa's south side, which treated arthritis patients. She got no relief there. The pain then started in her legs. Several years later, Marie went to Argonne National Laboratory to be studied along with other women who worked with radium. The doctors said her bones had a "honeycombed" pattern, a word used with several other former radium workers. However, they stubbornly refused to admit it was caused by radium.

Mary Vicini Tonielli.

Alma Whittaker.

Doctors in Peoria told her that her leg needed to be amputated. They said to go home and think about it. Marie replied, "Why think about it? Let's go. If it needs to be done, it needs to be done." Marie's determined personality got her walking with an artificial leg, and even dancing with her walker.

Patty Gray said, "She kept a really good outlook. She figured it happened. There was really nothing she could do about it. She was a fighter."

Marie later broke her other leg and was confined to a wheelchair, eventually moving to Ottawa Care Center. She did not slow down there. She organized activities and delivered mail.

Marie Rossiter died on November 25, 1993 of a heart ailment at the age of eighty-seven. She donated her body to science, saying, "Maybe it will help somebody else."

Catherine Donohue was born in Ottawa on February 4, 1903, to Maurice and Bridget (O'Connor) Wolfe. They lived at 917 Ontario Street, near the Fox River, in Ottawa. Her mother died in 1909; her father died of a lung ailment in 1913. Catherine went to live with an aunt and uncle, Mary and Winchester Biggart, at 520 E. Superior Street. Mary died in 1928; Winchester died in 1931.

Catherine worked at Radium Dial from 1922 to August 1931. Already sick by 1930, Catherine was promoted to a job where she weighed material for the dial painters and scraped material from the workers' trays using her fingernails. Other workers were sent for medical tests. Catherine asked manager Rufus Reed if she could also be tested because she was feeling badly. He said "no."

Marie Becker Rossiter's First Communion picture at St. Patrick's Catholic Church in Ottawa.

Next page: Marie Rossiter in her years at Radium Dial. In the top left picture, she is on Columbus Street across from the building. In the top right picture, she is in Washington Park, with the Appellate Court in the background.

MARIE

Marie and Patrick Rossiter at Starved Rock State Park.

Marie Rossiter.

Marie Rossiter worked in this F. W. Woolworth store in Ottawa in 1920, before working at Radium Dial and before her marriage. She is the ninth person from the front on the left. A sign says, "Nothing in this store over 10 cents."

Marie Rossiter.

PREVIOUS PAGE, BELOW:

Left: Marie Rossiter in her youth.

Right: Marie and her great-granddaughter, Molly Gonzalo.

TIMES Learns Ottawa Radium Firm Now in N.Y.

By VICTOR SHOLIS
(TIMES Staff Correspondent)

New York, July 8.—The Radium Dial Co., which allegedly "skipped out" of Ottawa, Ill., leaving nine women dead and 15 others doomed to horrible deaths of "radium" poisoning, was found here by the TIMES today doing business on New York's lower east side.

As in Ottawa, women and girls are employed in the company's plant, located at 114 E. 25th st. Whether they have been informed of the danger said to lurk in the "radium" paint used in their work, the TIMES, as yet, has been unable to ascertain.

One point, however, is established in the company's favor: Much greater precautions are being taken to afford protection to the workers than, according to the Ottawa victims' accounts, were taken when the company had its plant in the Illinois city.

Moreover, inquiry at the offices of the New York state industrial commission reveals

Mrs. Catherine Donahue

Mrs. Charlotte Purcell

Mrs. Pearl Payne

Mrs. Peter Byers

destroys the white corpuscle's of their blood in a sort of "industrial leprosy."

WORKING ON CODE

"We are working now on a code to protect employes engaged in this work," State Industrial Comr. Elmer Andrews said. "Morever, New York's occupational disease act is thoroughly up to date and such as to afford them maximum protection."

Illinois, until recently, had an entirely inadequate occupational disease act, finally declared unconstitutional by the state Supreme court. One of the reasons the doomed women of Ottawa have been unable

before the Illinois industrial commission in Ottawa July 25.

CLOSED ITS PLANT

But here, too, the out-of-date provisions of the old Illinois law tend to operate against them. The Radium Dial Co. "skipped out"—closed its plant in Ottawa—leaving a bond of only $10,000 posted with the industrial commission.

According to J. S. Cook, Chicago attorney who represented the doomed women in a test case, the concern now operating here in New York is a "new" corporation. The "old" corporation that operated the plant in Ottawa, Cook says, has been abandoned.

Legally, therefore, it would be im-

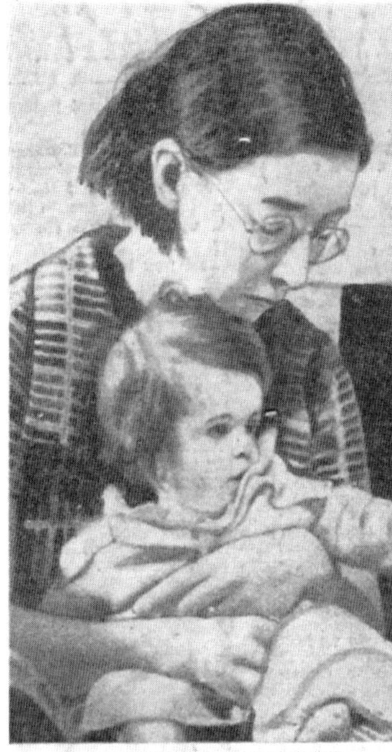
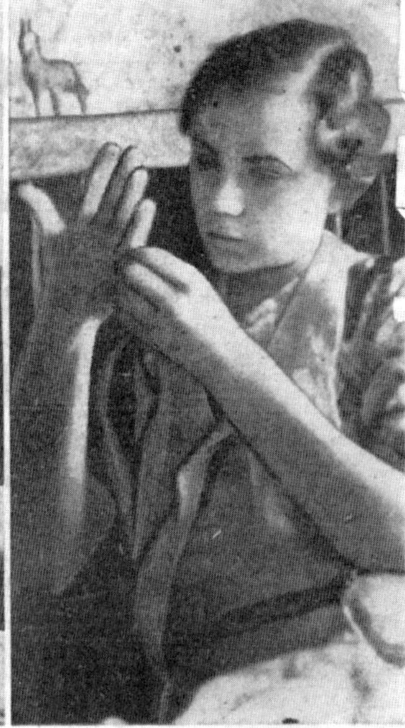

MRS. CATHERINE DONOHUE
Radium victim and daughter, Mary Jane.

MRS. MARIE ROSSITER
With eleven others, she counts months.

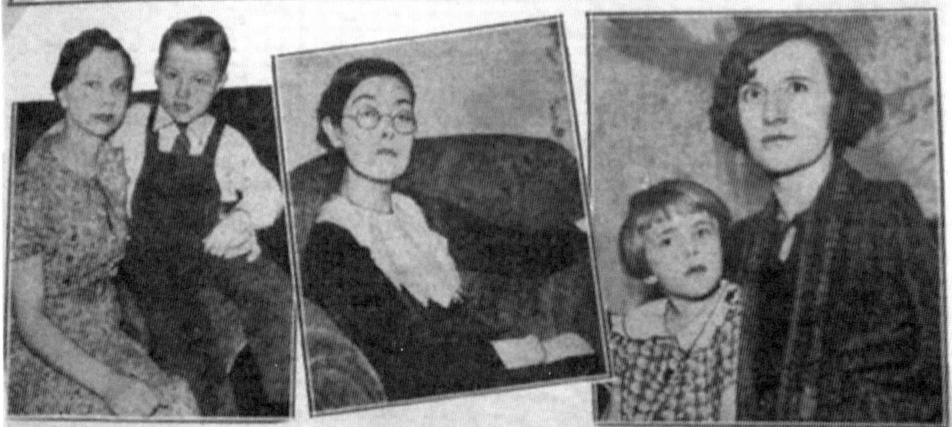

Mrs. Marie Rossiter and son, William.

Mrs. Catherine Donahue, mother of two children.

Mrs. Charlotte Purcell and daughter, Patricia.

[TIMES Photos]

These mothers are victims of radium poisoning contracted while working for Radium Dial Co. at Ottawa, Ill. Mrs. Rossiter is being treated for infected right ankle; Mrs. Donahue has one hip locked and disease has spread to ankle; Mrs. Purcell, mother of three children, has lost her left arm and doctors are fighting vainly to save other one.

Catherine no longer worked at Radium Dial when she married Tom Donohue on January 23, 1932. Rev. Dean Thomas Madden performed the ceremony at St. Columba Catholic Church. Her gown was canton crepe with a matching hat of straw, matching shoes and a bouquet of tea roses. Catherine Mulholland was maid of honor and Matthew Donohue was best man. A wedding breakfast was served to twenty-three guests at her home at 520 E. Superior Street before the couple left on a week's honeymoon.

Catherine was limping down the aisle to take her wedding vows. A few months after the wedding, Catherine began complaining of pain in her hip and in her jaw. By the spring of 1934, her health was failing dramatically. Her husband had to care for the children. The Donohues had two children: Thomas, Jr., born April 26, 1933, and Mary Jane, born November 20, 1934.

Tom Donohue was almost penniless, having lost his job at Libbey-Owens-Ford glass factory in Ottawa due to the Great Depression, as well as mortgaging his house to feed the family and to pay Catherine's medical expenses.

Tom Donohue ran into Rufus Reed on Columbus Street in Ottawa one day. Mr. Donohue confronted Mr. Reed about radium causing all the health problems. Charlotte Purcell and her husband, Al, walked out of the building at that time, and Al also started questioning Mr. Reed. Reed would have nothing to do with either man. A heated argument ensued. Mr. Donohue and Mr. Reed exchanged blows. Mr. Reed stumbled, and he called to a sheriff's deputy who happened to be nearby. Mr. Reed yelled, "He hit me!" The Donohue family story, according to great-nephew Ed Carroll, is that the sympathetic deputy replied, "All I saw was you tripping over your own feet." Rufus Reed did have Tom Donohue arrested, but the case was dropped.

Catherine Donohue told the *Chicago Herald and Examiner* in March 1936 that she first realized her true condition when her dentist said pulling a tooth would shatter her jawbone:

> My ankles and hips have become infected ... I am in constant pain. I have to take opiates to relieve it. I am virtually an invalid, but I must tell myself that I must live for my children. I am losing weight steadily and I cannot walk a block. But somehow I must carry on.

Mrs. Donohue cried when she told the reporter about the recent death of Inez Vallat. "I knew her when she was a picture of health. But when I saw her last, she was a living corpse, hobbling around like an old woman."

In the same newspaper story, Marie Rossiter said, "I'm frightened to death, but I want to live as long as I can for the sake of my little boy, Bill. There were ten of us girls in that one room. Four already are gone. Perhaps I'll be next. I can't help worrying about it."

Doomed to death by radium poisoning, Mrs. Catherine Donohue at Ottawa appears before Illinois Industrial commission, reopens battle for compensation from Radium Dial Co., in whose employ she contracted disease. First suit was outlawed by defunct law.—*Story on page 3.*

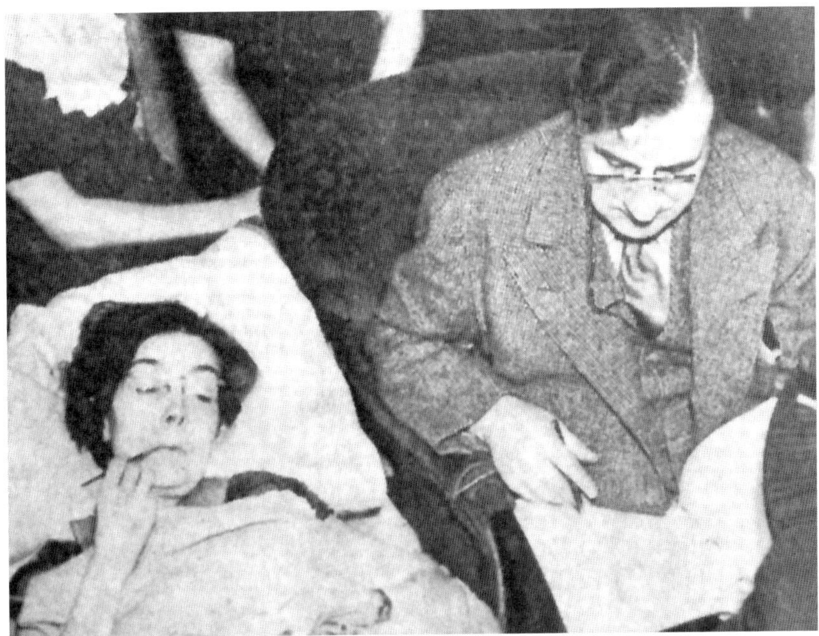

At the hearing before the Illinois Industrial Commission in February 1938, Catherine Donohue demonstrated for attorney Leonard Grossman how the women were instructed to put the paint brush tipped with radium to their lips to get a fine point on the brush. This was done hundreds of times each day. The second day of the hearing had to be held in the Donohue house because Catherine was too weak to get off her couch.

Catherine Donohue sitting in her living room.

Charlotte Purcell was quoted:

> We were a bunch of happy, vivacious girls. Many were simply beautiful, the brightest of the girlhood of Ottawa, Utica and adjoining towns. There were thirteen of us in a clique that worked together, danced together and had our outings along the river and at Starved Rock. At times, there were upward of 200 girls and women employed painting dials and hands.

Mrs. Donohue added:

> We were extremely happy in our associations until news of the poisonings and deaths from radium poisonings in Newark were printed. Then the girls became wild. There were meetings at the plant that bordered on riots. It is an awful thing for young girls just thinking of marrying and raising families to know they are doomed to early and horrible deaths ... The chill of fear was so depressing that we could scarcely work, scarcely talk of our impending fate.

A month before her agonizing death in 1938, Catherine Donohue wrote to the pastor of Our Lady of Sorrows Catholic Church in Chicago, asking that a novena be held for her benefit. She wrote:

> The doctors tell me I will die, but I mustn't. I have too much to live for—a husband who loves me and two children I adore. But the doctors say radium poisoning is eating away my bones and shrinking my flesh to the point where medical science has given me up as one of the living dead. They say nothing can save me, nothing but a miracle. And that's what I want, a miracle. If that is not God's will, perhaps your prayers will obtain for me the blessing of a happy death.

Catherine Donohue wrote several letters, which now are in the LaSalle County Historical Museum in Utica. She wrote to Pearl Payne on March 9, 1938:

> Am sitting up for a few minutes today and oh how good it feels after so long in bed. Several days ago, Sister Clara and Sister Michael of the convent brought me a relic of the true cross, which they rarely leave out. You know, Pearl dear, it is like having God in the house with me. I am to make a nine-day novena in honor of our dear Lord's sufferings. It rests in God's hands, dear! Pray for me, won't you.
>
> Olive was down to see me Sunday and brought me a chicken all cooked up lovely. She, like you dear, are truly pals, and may God bless you both.
>
> I grieved to hear you were not feeling well and do hope your old tooth ache is better, and was sure sorry you were not able to come up. Could you come Sunday if the weather is nice? Maxine was down and spent an evening with me. Have not heard from Charlotte in some time.
>
> How is your little girl and also your husband? Hope both are well. Tom is still at home with me. Work is very scarce in Ottawa. Write soon or come and see me, dear. Lots of love, Catherine.

Another letter was undated.

> My Dear Pearl, It has indeed been a long time since I have heard or seen any of you girls that it seems like writing to a stranger. I only wish we lived near one another. I have so much to say, one cannot just give it all on paper.

As to my health, I am still a cripple. As you remember, I was to take the x-ray treatment in Streator. Well, I took thirty of them and it sure failed to give me any relief. My hip is very bad, Pearl, it is all I can do to get around at all. I suffer so much pain that at times I feel as if life was pretty hard to bear.

Had a letter from Charlotte Purcell in Chicago. Her husband was over to see Grossman and he said he was trying to get something for us, but for God's sake, to get a doctor's statement. I have written my doctor for one and no reply came back. I don't know, Pearl, what is to be done. I only wish you folks could come up and see us before the 10th. As for details, there are none. Tom is not working now or I would call him long distance and find out if he is coming down the 10th. Seems funny he has not written, doesn't it?

'Living dead' asks miracle— Thousands go to Our Lady of Sorrows church today for novena services at which devout are asked to pray for a miracle for Catherine Donohue, "living dead woman" of Ottawa. In letter to Father James Keane, O.S.M., novena director, Mrs. Donohue asks prayers for her speedy recovery or happy death. (TIMES Photo) —Story on page 5.

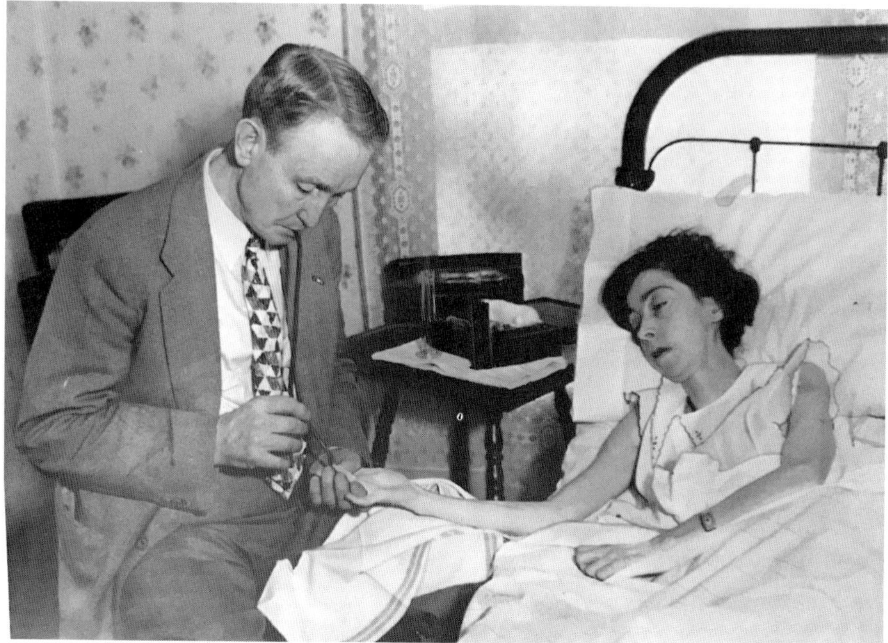

Dr. Charles Loffler gives Catherine Donohue a blood test.

The Donohue home at 520 E. Superior Street, Ottawa, in 1938 and 2019. The two-apartment house had a back yard that bordered the Illinois & Michigan Canal.

How are you all? Hope your husband is lucky in having work. It makes it bad around Xmas, but one mustn't complain. If you can drive up before the 10th, I would be glad. Best regards to you all from Thomas and I. Hoping to see you soon. Love, Catherine.

From her bed in St. Margaret's Hospital in Spring Valley, Catherine wrote to Pearl on May 1, 1938, asking Pearl to visit her. She wrote that she was "so lonesome away from home." "I suffer so much pain. Dr. wants to see what he can do to relieve it." She closed the letter, "How are you, dear? I do hope all is well with you. Come over if possible, won't you. As soon as you get this letter. I'm so lonesome and blue. Lots of love, Catherine."

Just days before her death, Catherine managed one last letter to Pearl, following the victory before the Illinois Industrial Commission:

Dear Pearl. Tried to write sooner but somehow I can't write any more, it is so difficult for me to sit up for any length of time, and when I do, I'm all in for a week afterwards. How are you dear! Hope all is well with you dear folks, as there is enough of us having trouble it seems.

Emma Engel has been here to see me. She and Marie Rossiter went to Chicago and had their x-ray pictures taken, and asked Marie Glacinski and Frances O'Connell to go with them, as they drove up, but that the girls refused to go. I'm really surprised, as it didn't cost much, $2.00 apiece, and Mr. Grossman took them to lunch. He is just about the best there is, isn't he?

I only wish my case was through with. God knows I need the medical care and need it badly. I'm sorry that things can't be different, but it was a wonderful victory so far.

Tom is working, but I don't think he feels so good. He doesn't say much but he is just wore out, it has been such a strain on him. God has sure blessed me with a good husband and lovely children. They are worth all the pain and suffering after all.

Olive was in to see me, she is such a dear, also. Brought me fruit and a pail of fresh eggs. Both of you have proven that one can still have faith in a few friends, real ones at heart, and it helps one along, dear, just to know someone thinks of him along life's way.

Hope Hobart is working, that the plant did not shut down. I know how hard it is to get along. Take care of yourself, dear, and don't worry. I shall pray for you all.

Tom sends his best regards and hope all will be well with you. Will let you know any news I hear. Am getting lovely letters from Canada, would sure love to see the papers.

Write soon, dear, and tell me all the news. Love, Catherine.

Olive Witt wrote to Pearl Payne on July 18, 1938:

I stopped in to see Catherine Saturday. Catherine had a bad spell the day before and had to have the doctor, but she was sitting up eating her lunch and she had on the pretty gown you gave her. She did look nice in it. Poor child. My heart goes out to her.

A few days before she died, a priest was called to give her the last rites of the church. "Is it that bad?" she asked her husband. He could not answer.

Catherine Donohue died at 2:52 a.m. on July 27, 1938, in her home. She was conscious until minutes before death, gaining comfort in the presence of her husband and two children.

Ottawa, Ill
March 9, 1908

Dearest Friend,

Am sitting up for a few minutes to day and oh how good it feels. after so long in bed. Several days ago Sister Clara and Sister Mildred of the convent brought me a relic of the true cross which they rarely lend out. You know Pearl dear it is like having God in the house with me. I am to making nine day novena in honor of our dear lord's sufferings. It rests in Gods hands dear. Pray for me wont you.

Alice was down to see me Sunday and brought me a chicken all cooked up lovely. She like you dear, are truly pals; and may God bless you both.

I grieved to hear you were not feeling well and do hope your old tooth ache is better and was sure sorry you were not able to come up. Could you come Sunday if the weather is nice? Mable was down to d. Spent an evening with me, have not heard from Charlotte in some time.

How is your little girl and do your husband? Hope both are well. Tom is still at home with me. Work is very scarce in Ottawa.

Write soon or come and see me dear.

Lots of love
Catherine

Dear Pearl.

Tried to write sooner but some how I cant write any more. it is so difficult for me to set up for any length of tyme and when I do I'm all in for a week afterwards.

How are you dear, hope all is well with you dear folks, as their is enough of us having trouble it seems.

Emma Engel has been here to see me Phil & Marie Kossitio went to Chicago and had their X-Ray pictures taken and asked Marie Glacinski and Francis O'Connell to go with them (as they drove up) but that the girls refused to go. I'm really suprised us at didn't cost much $2.00 a piece and Mr Grossman took them to lunch, He is just about the best their is, isn't he?

I only wish my case was through with, God knows I need the medical care and need it badly. I'm sorry that things can't be different but it was a wonderful victory so far.

Tom is working, but I don't think he

feels so good he doesn't say much but he is just worn out, itg has been such a strain on him. God has sure blessed me with a good husband and lovely children. They are worth all the pain and suffering after all.

Alice was in to see me, she is such a dear also. brought me fruit, and a pail of fresh eggs. Both of you have proven that one can still have faith in a few friends, real ones at least, and it helps one along dear just to know some one thinks of him along life's way.

Hope Hubert is working, that the plant did not shut down, I know how hard it is to get along. Take care of your self dear and don't worry I shall pray for you all.

Tom sends his best regards and hope all will be well with you. Will let you know any news I hear, am getting lovely letters from Canada, would sure love to see the papers.

Write soon dear and tell me all the news.

Love — Catherine.

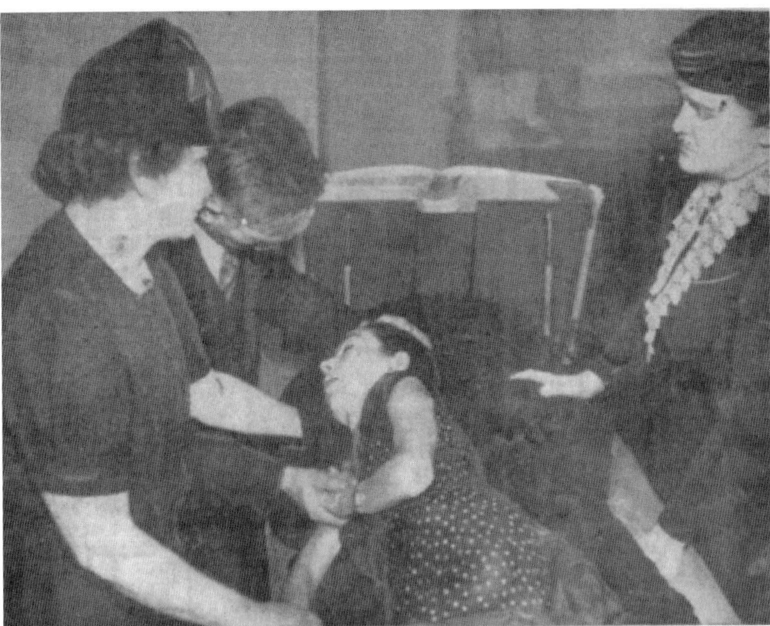

Don't Leave Me, Tom!' — Feebly quavering dramatic plea to husband, radium poison victim Mrs. Catherine Donohue lies stretched out in Ottawa county clerk's office after collapsing during compensation it against Radium Dial Co. By her side stands Mrs. Pearl Payne (left), another of Ottawa's "doomed women," suffering from dread disease. (AP Photo) (Story on page 3. Other pictures on pages 3, 34 and 35.)

These are some of the saddest newspaper clippings you will ever see, from the *Chicago Times*, as Catherine Donohue was slowly dying.

Radium victim dead — Sorrowing eyes raised to heaven, hands clasped in supplication, Tommy Donohue Jr. and sister Mary Jane kneel before crucifix in prayer for their mother, Catherine Donohue. She died yesterday, her body wracked by pains of radium poisoning contracted while working for Radium Dial Co. at Ottawa. Counsel seeks sweeping investigation into cause of her death. (TIMES Photo (C) 1938) —Story on page 3.

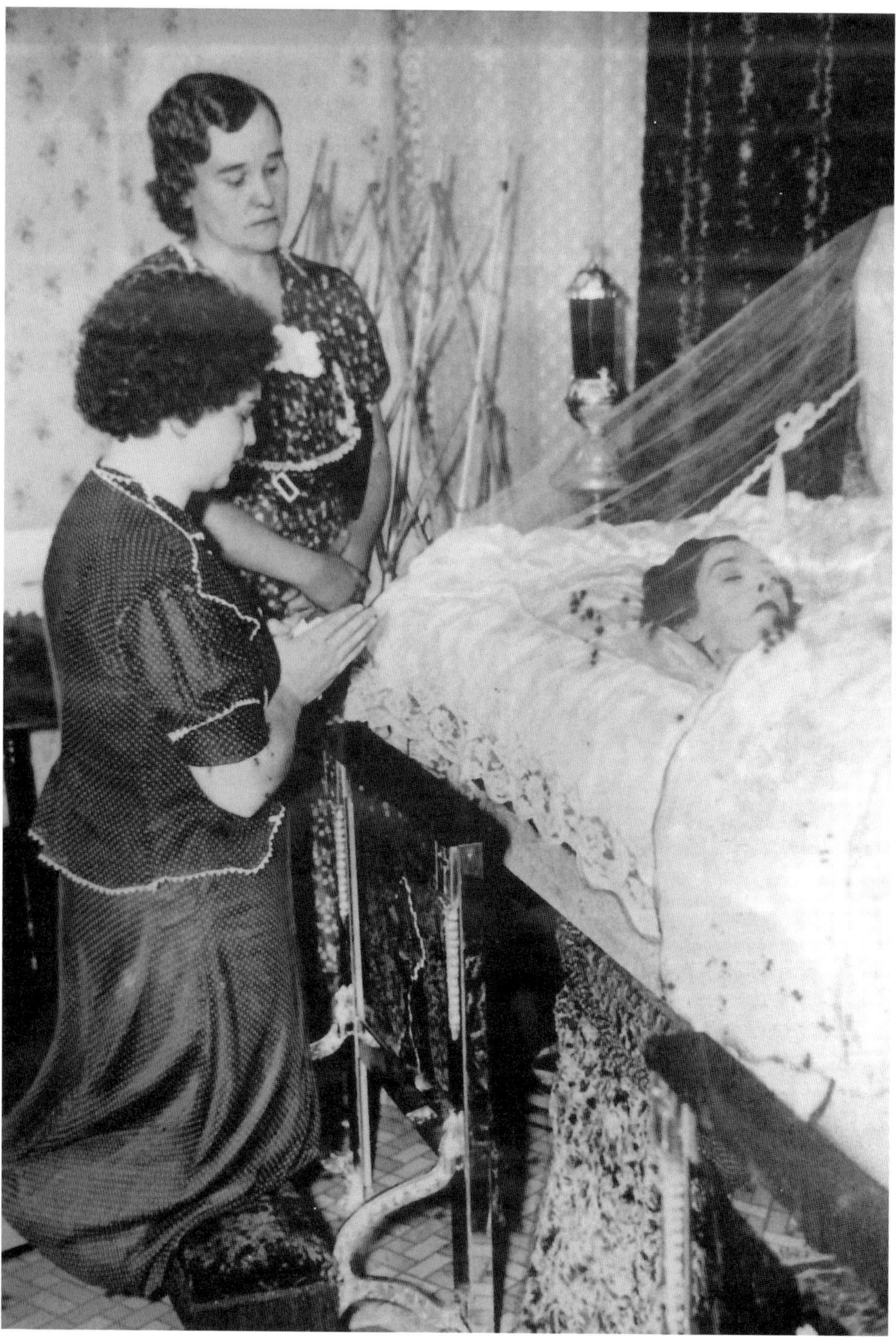

Pearl Payne kneels to pray before the casket of Catherine Donohue in the Donohue home on July 28, 1938.

Roll call of living— Other radium poison victims gather at Catherine Donohue's funeral. Same poison that killed Mrs. Donohue bombards their bones. Left to right are: Marie Rossiter, Pearl Paine, Romelda Bierman, Marguerite Glacinski and Helen Munch. —*Story on page 10.*

Mrs. Donohue's casket is borne from home in Ottawa where she died. Relatives and friends were pallbearers. (TIMES Photos)

Mourners wait outside the Donohue home, as the casket is carried out the front door to St. Columba Catholic Church down the street.

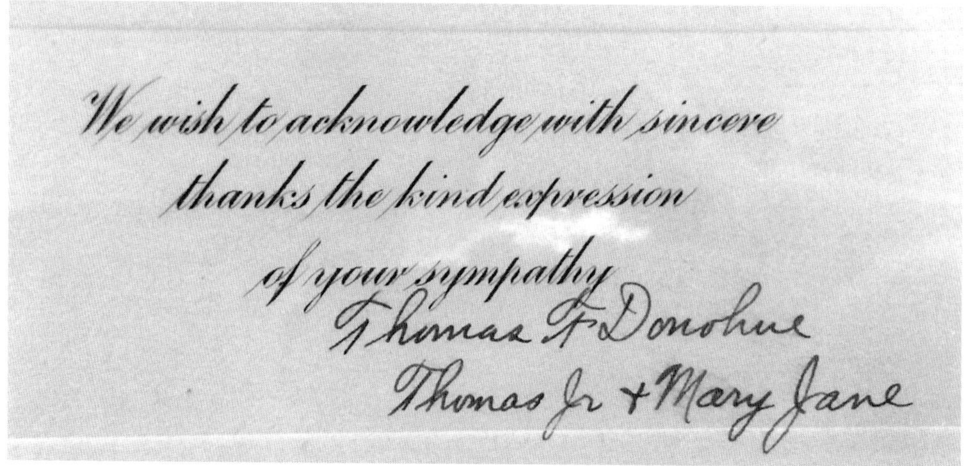

The Donohues thanked their friends for their support.

Catherine Donohue's grave in St. Columba Cemetery.

Hundreds of people came to her wake in her home at 520 E. Superior Street, and to her funeral at St. Columba Catholic Church on July 29.

The *Ottawa Daily Republican-Times* reported, "Her wasted body lay in a plain casket, in the shadow of a crucifix and tall candles, and surrounded by wreaths and garlands from friends and neighbors." Rev. James Griffin conducted the funeral mass. Pallbearers were Elmer Wolfe, Fred Bennett, James Wolfe, Joseph Mulholland, Owen Fox, and Thomas Donohue, a cousin of her husband,

The inquest was held the night before the funeral at the Gladfelter mortuary. The newspaper reported:

> A weary little man with gray hair, shaken with grief over the death of his wife and apparently bewildered by the ballyhoo and publicity that attended it, as well as her last illness, Thomas F. Donohue took the witness stand.

Mr. Donohue told his wife's story as detailed in this book.

Dr. Charles Loffler testified that had treated Mrs. Donohue for four years, and he said the cause of death was radium poisoning. Testimony from Dr. Walter Dalitsch was included in the record, which also asserted radium poisoning. Former dial painters Olive Witt, Pearl Payne, Marie Rossiter, Emma Engle, Helen Munch, and Margaret Glacinski were at the inquest. Leonard Grossman wanted them to testify, but the coroner, Dr. Harry Sterling Lester, said that was not necessary.

The coroner's jury ruled that Mrs. Donohue died of radium poisoning caused from her work at Radium Dial. The jurors were L. L. Bennett, Raymond Fast, Richard Mullen, James Armstrong, and Matt and James White.

Settlements with other women finally were reached in 1939. Charlotte Purcell got $350; Helen Munch got $100; and Frances O'Connell, Marguerite Glacinski, and Olive Witt got $25 each. The court allowed $783 for attorney fees, $1,506 for expenses of handling the lawsuit, and $1,900 for medical expenses.

Even though Mrs. Donohue had been awarded $2,442 plus $3,239 by the Illinois Industrial Commission, her estate was awarded only $1,200. Mr. Donohue had only $413 left from the settlement, after paying funeral expenses and other bills.

Argonne National Laboratory exhumed Catherine Donohue's body on October 2, 1984. Scientists examined the remains and returned her to St. Columba Cemetery on August 16, 1985. Unlike Peg Looney, she was not returned in a lead-encased casket. "There were just scraps left because her casket leaked," her great-nephew, Ed Carroll, told me.

Margaret "Peg" Looney was the eldest daughter of Michael and Ethel Looney, in an Irish-American family of ten children. She was born on December 20, 1904. She attended St. Xavier's Academy, a girl's high school, where her 1922 yearbook described her as a "bookworm with a voice ever so soft, gentle and low," who liked to giggle.

The family lived at 1850 Columbus Street, just south of the railroad tracks, between Jones and Fremont streets. It was quite a walk to Radium Dial at 1022 Columbus Street for Peg every day, but the family was too poor to afford a car.

Infamous gangster John Looney came back to Ottawa for occasional visits, but he never financially helped his poor cousins. John Looney grew up in Ottawa on East Marquette Street (in a house later owned by my in-laws. He was portrayed by Paul Newman in the 2002 film, *The Road to Perdition*).

Peg Looney started working at Radium Dial on January 1, 1923, when she was just seventeen. She earned $17.50 a week. When she had a tooth pulled in 1925, the wound did not heal. Her health took a dramatic downturn after that.

She tested positive for radium in 1925 and again in 1928. After both tests, the company lied and told her she was "the picture of health." Her jaw fractured and her condition continued to get worse. A specialist told her family that the bones in her face were "honeycombed" with radium and nothing could be done. She worked up until a week before she died, despite being in great pain.

Peg Looney collapsed at work on August 6, 1929. She was taken to what was called "the company hospital." It really was not the company hospital. Illinois Valley Hospital was run by Dr. Roswell Pettit, who was Radium Dial's local doctor. The facility was on Center Street on Ottawa's south side, where the tuberculosis sanitarium had been located. This later was the Arthritis Sanitarium, and then Ottawa General Hospital. It now is Ottawa Pavilion nursing home. Peg Looney died at that hospital on August 14. She was twenty-four years old.

Ethel Looney told the *Chicago Herald and Examiner* in March 1936, "She knew she had to go. You could see her slowly dying. There was nothing you could do. 'Well, Mother,' she used to say, 'my time is nearly up.' She worked until a few days of her death. Her death was a relief from suffering."

As soon as Peg Looney died, company officials tried to take her body in the middle of the night to bury the evidence. Jack White, who was Peg's brother-in-law, would not allow it. The family demanded a proper Catholic funeral.

"Jack was married to Peg's sister Catherine," Mary Bailey, Jack's niece, said. "He was a very nice and easy-going person. It was out of character for him to be so aggressive."

Radium Dial lawyers then promised that the Looney family's doctor could participate in the autopsy. However, Radium Dial had its own doctor, Aaron Arkin, conduct the autopsy on the same day Miss Looney died, before the family physician arrived. The family doctor did not get to examine the body.

The company doctor's report said there was no issue with the teeth, gums, or jaw, and the spleen, gastro-intestinal tract, peritoneum, kidneys, ureter, adrenals, and pancreas all were normal. The doctor listed diphtheritic pharyngitis, laryngitis, edema of the glottis and epiglottis, bronchopneumonia and dilation of the heart as the cause of Peg Looney's death, not radium.

Dr. Arkin's four-page report claimed there was "no evidence of necrosis or osteomyelitis," and "sections from the upper jaw reveal normal bone tissue." Dr. Arkin omitted any mention of the lower jaw because he had stolen it from her corpse.

In plain terms, diphtheria is a bacterial infection in the throat. Pharyngitis is an inflammation or infection of mucus membranes of the passageway from the nasal cavity to the larynx. Edema is an excess of fluids in the tissues. The glottis is the back of the tongue; the epiglottis is the upper cartilage of the larynx. Necrosis is the death of cells. Osteomyelitis is inflammation of the bones and marrow. None of those "causes" were attributed to radium.

Miss Looney's autopsy was observed by Dr. Pettit, a nationally known physician who had founded the tuberculosis "tent colony" and hospital, and by Dr. Joseph O'Neill and by Dr. William Blue, who listed himself as an oculist and aurist. They diagnosed diphtheria as the cause of death.

Jack White is on the far right at the May 27, 1939, wedding of his brother, Edward, to Juanita LaValle. Mary Landers is the maid of honor.

Margaret Looney's plain grave marker in St. Columba Cemetery.

#242529

Chicago, ILL. Aug. 27. 1929

The Radium Dial Company
25 E Washington St.,
Chicago, ILL.

Gentlemen;

  We hand you, herewith, report on autopsy performed on the body of Miss margaret Looney, Ottawa, ILL.,at your request on August 14,1929. This autopsy was performed at the Dwyer Undertaking parlor Ottawa Ill., by our Dr. Aaron Arkin.

EXTERNAL APPEARANCE:

  The body is that of a young woman 5 feet 3 inches in height. There is little subcutaneous fat, the patient weighing about 100 pounds. There is no evidence of an external injury or laceration of the skin. The skull appears normal. The teeth are in excellent condition. The gums appear normal. There is no ulceration of the gums, nor any evidence of any destructive bone changes in the upper or lower jaw. The chest is symmetrical. There is no evidence of any injury of the chest wall. The extremities appear normal,

INTERNAL EXAMINATION:
  On opening the thorax, no evidence of pleurisy or an excess amount of fluid in the pleural cavity is noted. The pleura appears normal. The upper lobes of the lung appear normal. There is a disseminated bronchopneumonia in both lower lobes, expecially the right. It is in the red hepatization stage.

  The trachea contains a considerable amount of frothy fluid and some mucus. There is some fluid, also, in both main bronchi.

  In the pharynx there is a typical diphtheritic membrane, which covers the lower portion of the pharynx. Its upper border is rather sharply outlined. It extends to the region of the glottis and epiglottis. The membrane consists of a fibrinous necrotic exudate which can be removed with difficulty. There is a very marked edema of the glottis and, also, of the epiglottis. The epiglottis is about 5 times the normal thickness. The vocal cords are,also,markedly edematous. The result is a very narrow laryngeal orific

  The pericardium appears normal. There is a normal amount of fluid. There is a slight enlargement of the heart. There is no evidence of valvular disease. The aortic, mitral, tricuspid and pulmonary valves all appear normal.

  The peritoneal cavity is filled with a formaline-containing fixing fluid,which was injected after the embalmin.The liver appears normal except for

The first page of a four-page autopsy report from a Chicago laboratory on Margaret Looney.

Margaret "Peg" Looney is shown in this photograph of four generations of her family. Standing in the back is her mother, Ethel (McComber) Looney. On the left is her great-grandmother, Mary Green. On the right is her grandmother, Hannah Jane Burke.

Peg Looney and Charles Hackensmith are flanked by Peg's sisters: Edith on the left and Theresa on the right. Margaret's last sister, Jeanette Schott, died on October 18, 2019, at the age of ninety-five. Ironically, she died in Ottawa Pavilion nursing home, the same "company hospital" facility where Margaret had died ninety years earlier.

MARGARET LOONEY.

A Voice ever soft, gentle and low.

Peg is one of the survivors of the Freshman Class of 1918, having come to S. X. A. from St. Columba's, Ottawa. In quantity she is lacking, but not in quality. "For Silence is Golden." Margaret believes in being first to pay all debts, and first to take all "Exams"!

Margaret Looney's high school yearbook picture at St. Xavier's Academy.

The Sisters of Mercy came to Ottawa from Ireland in 1859 and founded St. Joseph's Convent and St. Xavier's Academy. This building, at Washington and Paul streets, was completed in 1900. It became a girl's school in 1913. The name was changed to Ottawa Catholic High School in 1946 when both boys and girls were admitted. The name was changed to Marquette High School in 1949. This building was replaced with a newer one in the 1950s.

A story in the *Ottawa Daily Republican-Times*, written by a Radium Dial spokesman, said:

> The young woman's physical condition for a time was puzzling. She was employed at the Radium Dial studio, and there were rumors her condition was due to radium poisoning. In order that there might be no doubt as to the cause of death, there was an autopsy. Dr. Aaron Arkin said there was no doubt that death was caused by diphtheria. There was no visible indication of radium poisoning.

This lie was told even though the company had the 1928 tests that showed more than half the workforce of sixty-seven women were radioactive. The highest levels were in Margaret Looney, Mary (Vicini) Tonielli, Marie (Becker) Rossiter, and Catherine (Wolfe) Donohue.

The Looney family wanted to file a lawsuit against the company, but no lawyer in Ottawa would take the case because the official cause of death was listed as diphtheria, not radium poisoning.

For years, Ethel Looney would walk several miles to visit her daughter's grave every day. Ethel died in 1975 at the age of ninety-one.

Peg Looney had been engaged to Charles Hackensmith. As Peg declined in health, he would pull her around the neighborhood in a wagon so she could visit friends. By that time, she was unable to walk. However, she still went to work.

Charles went on to earn a doctorate and he became an author and a professor at the University of Kentucky. Yet he never got over Peg's death. Peg's niece, Darlene Halm, said Chuck wrote to the family for decades, up until his death in 1974. His wife, Lucinda, told the Looneys that she always knew when it was the anniversary of Peg's death because Charles would get quiet and sad.

After Luminous Processes became an issue in 1977, Peg Looney's body was exhumed by scientists at Argonne National Laboratory. Argonne reported her jaw was "honeycombed" with radioactivity. Nearly fifty years after her death, her grave still gave off enough radiation to be picked up by a Geiger counter. "The body was removed from the casket and taken away," Mrs. Halm said. "The casket and gloves were left at the cemetery for disposal by the grave diggers. Later that day, two of my aunts returned and saw the casket left by a water spigot." Her bones were found to still be highly radioactive, with 19,500 microcuries of radiation, more than a thousand times above the level considered safe. The bones were returned to St. Columba Cemetery six months later, in a lead-encased coffin.

Argonne's 1977 report noted Peg Looney's 1926 X-rays and blood tests, and that a tooth extraction never healed. It said, "Destruction of the bone tissue developed and the jaw bone was honeycombed, and this condition never cleared up." It noted this was contradictory to Dr. Arkin's autopsy report, which showed normal bone tissue from the upper jaw and no necrosis.

It added the previously unreleased information that Miss Looney was sent to the University of Chicago clinic for examination after a 1928 radium test and was told by doctors to change her employment.

Pearl (Konzal) Payne was born on March 8, 1900, in LaSalle, the eldest of thirteen children of Polish immigrants. She left school after the sixth grade to work as a nurse maid to a local banker. She went to night school, eventually earning a degree in nursing. She worked in a Chicago hospital until quitting to take care of her mother who was "taxed by the care of a family of thirteen children." She married Hobart Payne at the age of twenty-one, and they moved to Utica, Illinois. They had a daughter in March 1928.

Pearl Payne wrote about her own experiences. It is lengthy, but we feel it is necessary to include here because it is an important narrative of what a dial painter was suffering at the time. Her

Unidentified Ottawa dial painters, courtesy of LaSalle County Historical Museum in Utica.

Unidentified dial painters, courtesy of LaSalle County Historical Museum.

Previously unpublished photographs of unidentified dial painters outside the Radium Dial building. It is sad to think that these carefree young women were being poisoned by the jobs they loved without ever realizing what was happening to them every day. (*Photos courtesy of Patty Gray*)

St. Columba Catholic Church in Ottawa—the parish of Margaret Looney, Catherine Donohue, Charlotte Purcell, Marie Rossiter, Ella Cruse, Frances Glacinski, Mary Duffy, and many other Radium Dial workers—was located across the street from the Radium Dial Company building.

hand-written letters are in the LaSalle County Historical Museum in Utica. Pearl started work at Radium Dial in September 1923 and remained there for eight months. She wrote:

We were taught to keep the brushes pointed by placing them between the lips.

During the year of 1929 I began to feel ill, and got to the point where I staggered when I walked and had to be assisted up and down stairs ... I consulted Dr. R. L. Elliston, then of LaSalle, Illinois. He placed me in the hospital and treated me for about three weeks. I was sick the greater part of 1929. In fact, never became normal during that year. I had pains in (my) back and abdomen throughout the fall of 1929, during which time the doctor was urging me to submit to an operation. About Jan. 3, 1930, I entered the People's Hospital of Peru, where Drs. L. B. and R. L. Elliston performed an extensive abdominal operation.

Among other work performed at that time, a tumor was removed from the abdominal cavity. Three days after the operation, the parotid glands of the jaws of my face became affected. My head became swollen to twice its normal size. This condition persisted for about two months, at which time a head specialist was called in and he made an incision on the inside of each ear for drainage. The doctors then made an incision on the outside behind each ear and this healed so fast it had to be opened up every few days. During this time, my eyes became infected and an eye doctor had to be called in to treat the eyes. After two months in the hospital, I was released and one side of my face was paralyzed. Since that time, the paralysis left. From that time on, I was in poor health.

In Dec. 1931, I was bedridden with a persistent uterine hemorrhage for several weeks. And a curettement of the womb was performed. I returned home from the hospital and was continually in poor health. In June 1932, I again submitted to an abdominal surgical operation. Another tumor was removed and a curettement of the womb performed. Again about Dec. 1932 a uterine hemorrhage started and continued for several weeks. The Dr. was perplexed and said I must have been pregnant and had a miscarriage. I again returned to the hospital and Dr. performed another curettement in the womb. The Dr. persisting in the argument each time that I had been pregnant and possibly a miscarriage had taken place. I knew then it was not so. Because nothing had been done to cause me to be pregnant.

The doctor gave me a course of treatment for malaria fever with no results. At the time he had a blood count made and found I was in a badly anemic condition. I began to take a highly concentrated food for this condition. About April of 1933, I noticed that the hemorrhages were starting. This persisted for several weeks. I notified my doctor and he advised the removal of the uterus. I refused and lay in bed for several days debating what to do. At this time, I called in Dr. L. B. Griswold of Utica, Illinois. I gave him my history and he said I was in no condition to have an operation and that it might be fatal. It was, he said, impossible to make an examination until the hemorrhage was reduced. He placed me in bed and for several weeks tried to stop the hemorrhaging with internal medicines.

He succeeded in reducing long enough to make an examination. After which time the hemorrhage continued to get worse. In fact, it lasted eighty-seven days. He called in Dr. C. S. Capp of the University of Chicago who was substituting for Dr. Pettit of Ottawa, who was in Europe at the time. Dr. Capp rushed me to Ryburn-King Hospital in Ottawa, Illinois, believing I would have to have a blood transfusion, but instead gave me a course of x-ray treatments. This was about July 1933. I was there about seven days and then sent home to bed hoping the hemorrhaging would cease. But it continued.

About the latter part of July 1933, I was taken to the Illinois Valley X-ray Laboratory in Ottawa, Illinois. I was put under an anesthetic there and completely sterilized with x-ray and radium rays. After, I was brought home to bed, and in a few weeks the hemorrhage ceased. I remained in bed several months and was attacked by severe heart and sinking spells. The Dr. began administering a blood tonic, and later a gland substance which was to replace that manufactured by the abdominal glands that had been destroyed by tumors. This substance I will have to take the remainder of my life.

A premature change of life has been brought in by sterilization and all my illness has weakened my heart to such an extent that I am unable to do the work or conduct myself as an ordinary person should. My nervous system is also affected so that I am unable to enjoy life as a normal person should. The expense incurred was such that it will take years to straighten out.

Several years ago, it came to my attention that the girls that formerly worked at the Radium Dial Co. were dying prematurely and of mysterious causes. I began to investigate and found others yet living and in the prime of life were affected with ailments. After recalling the perplexities of the doctors in my past illnesses and the statement of one of them, quote, "That I belong to a class of women of which the medical profession does not know the reason for their illness."

I then began at this time to become of the firm opinion that my illness was due to radium poisoning. There may be some discrepancy in the dates as I have set down, but serves to show that I have reason to believe that compensation is due me (on) account of Illness contracted from previous employment from the Radium Dial Co. of Ottawa, Illinois.

There is something else I wish to state, due to the fact that I have had nursing experience. I know that neither myself or husband has no history of venereal disease. Also in my married life I never in any way ever tried or prevented conception. Hence, there was no cause for hemorrhages.

A prescription from Dr. Dalitsch to Pearl Payne, March 1938.

Pearl wrote this letter to her husband from her bed in People's Hospital in Peru, Illinois, on June 15, 1932:

Dearest Sweetheart, I love you and I am laying here thinking of you and wishing I was in your dear arms. I am afraid I was very impatient with you for some time, and I am heartily sorry. Please forgive me, as I have been very nervous and ill for a long time. Beneath it all I have loved you very deeply and dearly. You and my baby girl are two of my dearest possessions in this world. Pray for me daily, that I may get well perfectly. If not, do not grieve, as we must bow our heads to the Lord's will. Prayers and time will heal your sorrow some. Be good to our baby girl, teach her to love and remember me and above all, to be a good virtuous girl. Tell her I loved her dearly. Kiss and hug her each day for me. In time, teach her to pray for me. Oceans of love, hugs and kisses to both of my dearest and sweetest darlings. Pearl.

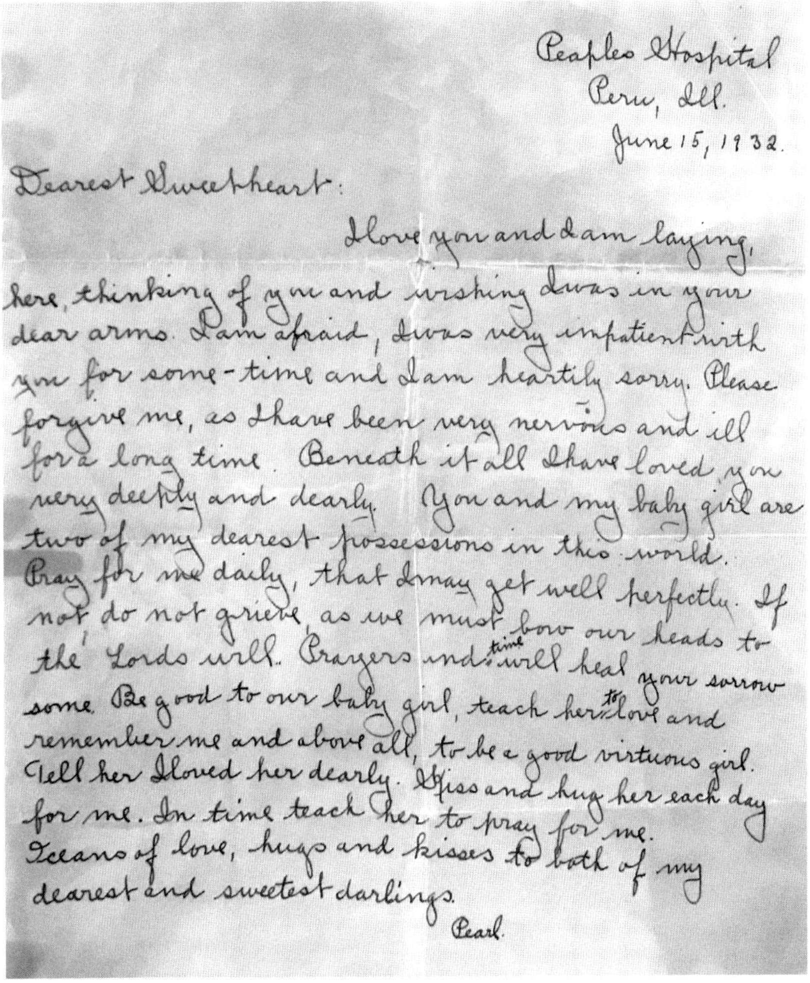

Pearl Payne's letter to her husband.

Pearl Payne, pictured during a spell of illness in 1933.

Next page: Pearl Payne's letter to her attorney, Leonard Grossman.

La Salle, Ill.
Feb 23, 1938.

Leonard Grossman
134 North La Salle St.
Chgo. Ill.

Dear Mr. Grossman:-

Sensing your humanitarian zeal for helping those on the lower rungs of life's ladder. And spurred by the many missals and statements of approval of your efforts. It has occured to me as well as th' other participant in the Radium Dial suit. That you use your great humanitarian instinct to forge the beginning of a society whereby those—of which there must be thousands—could band together, secure legal aid of a very competent nature and in general use our organized pressure to simplify, promote

②

and improve the laws relative to those who are maimed, and the recipients of ill health due to occupational hazards.

At a great sacrifice you have continued daily to lay other engagements aside, to formulate the great mass of information necessary to properly present these cases to the courts of our land. No less a compliment can also be paid to the efforts of your loyal secretary. And your wife who has sacrificed I am sure your association at times when you otherwise should have been at home.

Hoping this letter will be another stepping stone for your greater efforts and humanitarian ~~efforts~~ idealism I choose to remain,

A greatful client,

Pearl C. Payne

PHONE RANDOLPH 2026

LEONARD J. GROSSMAN

ATTORNEY AT LAW

SUITE 1800 CHICAGO REAL ESTATE BOARD BLDG.

32 WEST RANDOLPH STREET

CHICAGO

June 1st, 1938.

Mrs. Pearl Payne,
LaSalle, Illinois.

Dear Mrs. Payne:

Sorry I did not get a chance to write
to you sooner, but we have been extremely busy.

On Sunday, June 5th, we will be in Ottawa,
Illinois, and will expect to see you at four
o'clock P.M. at the home of Catherine Donohue.
On Monday morning, it will be necessary for you
to meet us at the Ottawa Hotel at ten o'clock.
The case of Catherine Donohue will be heard at
the City Hall of LaSalle, Illinois on Monday
afternoon. Best wishes.

Yours truly,

LEONARD J. GROSSMAN

cr

PHONE RANDOLPH 2026

LEONARD J. GROSSMAN

ATTORNEY AT LAW

SUITE 1800 CHICAGO REAL ESTATE BOARD BLDG.

32 WEST RANDOLPH STREET

CHICAGO

October 15, 1938.

Mrs. Peal Payne,
Utica, Illinois.

Dear Mrs. Payne:

    Received your very lovely card a few days ago and am terribly sorry I did not get to write you girls sooner, but have been busy day and night, working on the Radium case. Just recently we have completed two briefs which have been filed in the Supreme Court of Illinois, inanswer to Radium Dial's Co. petitions for leave to file a Writ of Error and Mandamus. We expect to have further word on this by the end of this month and will write you again. If the light prevails like I think it should in Springfield it will be carried to Washington, D. C. by Radium Dial Company, as they are laying the foundation in Springfield to take the case to the Supreme Court of the United States.

    God bless you and my heart is for you and I am happy to be in this fight for you and may be one of you can see some light as to how there can be some help forthcoming towards these continous expenses, which thus far I have had to bear. I trust this letter finds you cheerful and as well as may be expected. With kind and cordial greetings to your dear ones in which Mrs. Grossman and Carol join,

Yours truly,

Leonard J. Grossman

LEONARD J. GROSSMAN

PHONE RANDOLPH 2026

LEONARD J. GROSSMAN

ATTORNEY AT LAW

SUITE 402

134 NORTH LA SALLE ST.

CHICAGO

Top row: Marie Rossiter, Norma DeGroot, Catherine Donohue, and Charlotte Purcell.
Bottom row: Pearl Payne, Jeanette Byers, Marguerite Glacinski, and Helen Munch.

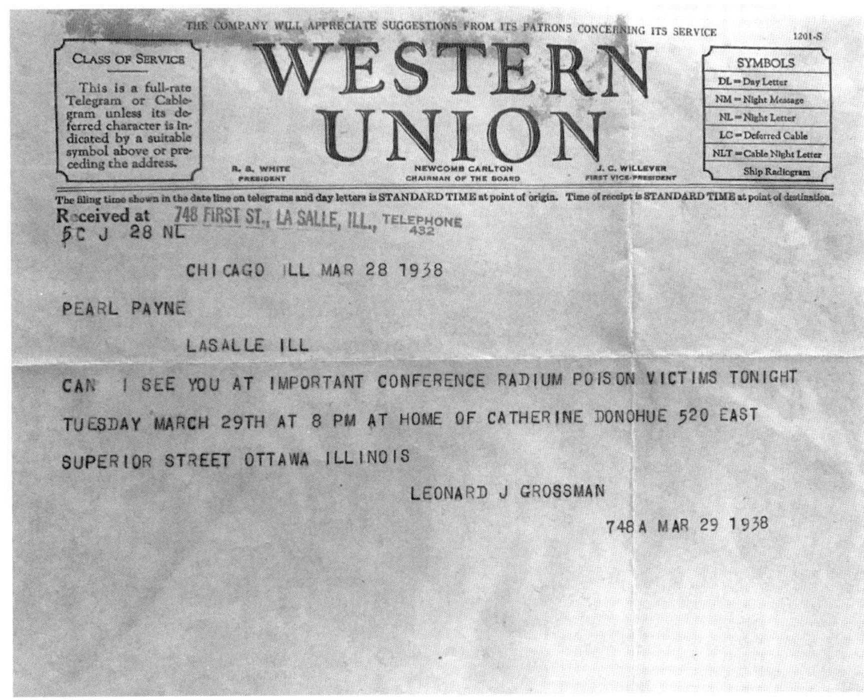

Telegram from Leonard Grossman to his clients, March 28, 1938.

ARTHUR H. COLWELL
LAWYER
508 CENTRAL LIFE BUILDING
OTTAWA, ILLINOIS

June 11, 1938

Dear Pearl:

Here is the Miraculous Medal and booklet I told you about and I would suggest all of you girls (I will tell those here when I see them, or if you write to them) to write to Father Keene of Our Lady of Sorrows Church, Chicago, Illinois, to place their names on the altar there at his church and then all of you could listen over WCFL every Friday evening at 9:00 our time (Central Standard) and I am sure all of you will benefit greatly and MIRACLES do happen even in this day and age Pearl, so don't give up hope and I feel all of you with the exception of Catherine, will come out on TOP.

Good bye Pearl and I hope to see you or hear from and have you tell me you are no longer worried.

Love,

Catherine O'Donnell

Catherine O'Donnell
1817 N. Columbus Street
Ottawa, Illinois

This card and medal are what you get when you send 25¢ for each membership. This card is mine but I don't need it, so I am passing it on to you. My name is registered there as a member and that is sufficient for me.

Finally, Gloria Boone's heart-rending comments can be understood by anyone who lost a mother:

My mother, Madeline Meany Berkley, worked there and died of the poisoning. She was thirty-eight years old and left four children and a husband. I was the youngest, and only two years old when she died, so I don't have any memories of her. I was told what a wonderful kind soul she was. Jim, I can't believe how painful it was to grow up without a Mother. I dreaded Mother's Day. My father remarried when I was three, but I was never considered her daughter. It was painful growing up and watching everyone around me with their mothers. There was a period in my very young life that I thought I was Cinderella, and that is what life is without your mother. No one hugged me or told me they loved me. My sisters did what they could, but were young themselves and didn't want the responsibility of me. I am seventy-five years old and I still carry the hole in my heart that only a mother could fill. Every time I think of Luminous Processes, I get angry. They are responsible for my mother's death and my lonely life of crying inside for my Momma.

8

LUMINOUS PROCESSES, 1934

Things began to get hotter than a radioactive isotope for Joseph Kelly, Sr., in Ottawa in 1934. Women had been dying from the working conditions at Radium Dial, but what was worse for the company was that the workers and the public learned about it and became frightened and outraged. The company did not seem to be willing to do anything about the problem, except to deny it.

Other historical accounts report that Radium Dial closed its doors in 1937, renamed itself Luminous Processes, and set up shop in a new building a few blocks away, at the corner of Jefferson and Clinton streets. That is close, but not exactly the truth.

Joseph Kelly, Sr., was ousted as Radium Dial's president in 1934, reportedly because of a stock fraud scheme. He and his son, Joseph Kelly, Jr., started Luminous Processes Incorporated that same year. Luminous Processes competed with Radium Dial for two years, even hiring some of the women away from Radium Dial.

Luminous Processes, 801 Clinton Street, Ottawa.

Radium Dial continued until it voluntarily went out of business in December 1936 to avoid legal liability. There were more "Radium" companies of various names created by the Kellys, all connected, and all designed to deflect financial liability from the original Radium Dial Company. Under the law, the new company, Luminous Processes, could not be held financially responsible for what another company, Radium Dial, did—even though both companies had the same owners.

The Ottawa Chamber of Commerce helped Luminous Processes find its location. Robert E. Turner, a company vice president who had been a manager at Radium Dial, became manager of Luminous Processes in Ottawa in 1934. The Ottawa newspaper said the building was "spacious, with comfortable work chairs and tables, modern lighting, arrangements and pleasant surroundings. The company maintains offices in New York and Chicago."

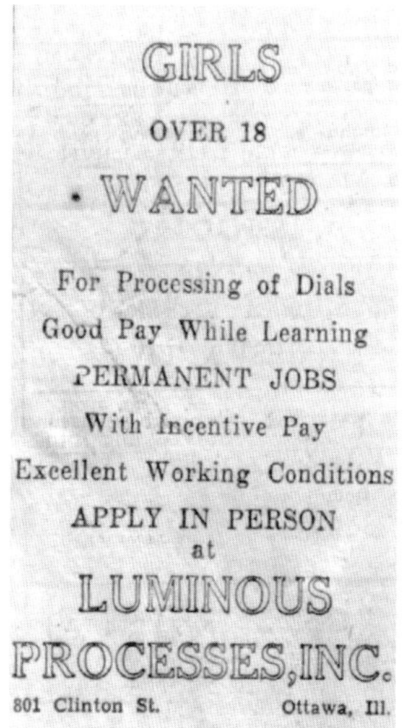

Above: Ottawa Daily Republican-Times, April 13, 1946.

Below: Luminous Processes workers, 1940s.

Everyone knew Luminous Processes was the same thing with just a different name. However, it was the depths of the Great Depression and women needed to work. People who are starving usually do not ask too many questions when offered an opportunity to feed their families.

The work of painting dials never stopped. The women were assured that the new procedures were safe. It was the same assurance the company gave when it told the women to put the brush tip to their tongues. The women believed them.

Luminous Processes, March 21, 1935: Vivienne Bekler, Dorothy Lambert, Edna Mae Krantz, Helen Morrison, Jane Clayton, Marjorie Hubert, Jean McGill, Elizabeth Smith O'Grady, Cassy DeFore, Lillian Smith Williams, Frances Pollack, Delores McCullough Joy, Dorothy Monroe, Mildred Nelson Moe, Zelma Kates, Margaret Westoff, Mable Lewis Williams, Emma Peppler, Helen Kammerer, E. Mae Dougherty, Margaret Webber, Alice Walsh, Marie Wieden, Geneva Mason, Ethel DeFore Joy, Bernice Browne Callahan, Alberta Hetrick, Emma Carroll, Doris Hetrick, LaVon Stafford, Ruth Ashbee, and Bertha Lanter.

Luminous Processes, April 21, 1936. Row 1: Mildred Moe, Jean McGill Hubert, Dolores M. Joy, Emma Carroll, Alberta Hetrick, Mable Lewis Williams, and Irene Shepard. Row 2: Zelma Schendawalt Caates, Dorothy Lambert, Margaret Westcott, Emma Weber Peppler, Frances Pollock, Helen Murphy Morrison, Edna Daugherty, Ann Carpenter Arthur, Lillian Smith Williams, Doris Hetrick Schwermacher, Dorothy Doer, Georgia Hanlon, Jewel Mason Kranz, Alma Bagley, Bob Bischoff, and Burton Safious. Row 3: Frances Schomas, Agnes Ollie, Margaret Geiger, Evelyn Houtchins, Mayme Loeb, Arla Engle, Alice Walsh, Felicia Madis Reeder, Bertha Lanter, Ruth Ashbee, LaVon Stafford, Mildred Over, Dorothy McGinnis, Dorothy Monroe, Jane Clayton, Violet Rigg, and Elda Horan. Row 4: Catherine Callahan, Bernice Browne Callahan, Marie Weeden, Ethel Defore Jones, Geneva Mason Costello, Lena Beldown, Cassie Defore Ball, Margaret Weber, Marjorie Hubert Knutson, Evelyn Fraiken, Edna Mae Kranz, and Mary Peppler.

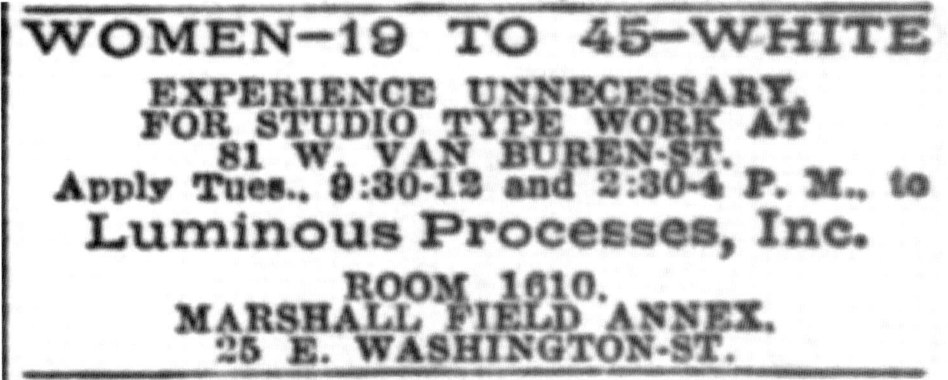

This picture was taken in 1936. You can always tell the difference between the Radium Dial and Luminous Processes studios—Luminous Processes had lower ceilings, and windows with the lower half-covered with a green frosting.

Luminous Processes advertised for workers in the Marshall Field annex at 25 E. Washington Street in Chicago in 1942 to meet the military's demands for luminous dials in its aircraft. The company advertised for white women, ages nineteen to forty-five.

Photographs of Luminous Processes by the Sheffel Studio of Ottawa in the 1930s and 1940s.

9

LUMINOUS PROCESSES, 1978

The Luminous Processes story is a case of history repeating itself because some people did not pay close enough attention the first time. Luminous Processes picked up where Radium Dial had left off in the 1930s—painting dials, endangering women, and taking no responsibility.

In 1975, Luminous Processes switched from using radium (which was regulated by the state) to tritium (which was regulated by the federal Nuclear Regulatory Commission). Tritium is a radioactive form of hydrogen and it replaced radium paint on clock dials.

It was when the company came under federal inspection that it began to have problems. The NRC suspended the license of Luminous Processes on February 17, 1978, after a January 31 inspection showed unsafe levels of tritium and a failure to clean up contaminated areas. The NRC had fined Luminous $3,250 after two failed inspections in 1976 and 1977. Luminous Processes was given twenty days to reply to the suspension order.

I was a reporter for *The Daily Times* in Ottawa at that time. A few days after the license was suspended, I wrote my first story on the subject for newspaper. At the time, Luminous Processes employed thirty-five workers. I contacted a number of those workers and found that several of those women had contracted breast cancer and other cancers. Of the dozen women who spoke to me, seven had surgery for breast cancer, one had a blood disease, and a few had other tumors.

One of the women who spoke to me in February and March 1978 was Mary Corrigan, who had worked for Luminous Processes for thirty-six years. She was getting treatment for breast cancer. I asked her if she thought the lack of safe procedures caused the tumors of many of the workers. She said yes. "We realized it was dangerous, but we were never told the whole facts of it." Miss Corrigan died on December 14, 1978. She was fifty-eight years old.

Pearl Schott, who had breast cancer, said the workers were told to be careful with the tritium because it was expensive, but they were not told to be careful because it was dangerous. Mrs. Schott worked there thirty-two years, until 1978. She said that fans kept the air moving in the factory during sweltering summer days, and it also blew radium dust all around.

Martha Hartshorn worked there from 1947 to 1978. She said the company would let women take small jars of radium home. They painted objects at home to make them glow. Other women at that time did not want to be identified because they were negotiating for severance and vacation pay that they were owed.

The women said that safety precautions were lax. One woman told me the superintendent "slapped the tritium around like cake frosting." The managers cared more about production than about worker safety, she said.

When the plant changed from radium to tritium, the workers were told tritium was harmless. However, they became scared of the smell in the plant, and they said tritium gas caused marks on their skin. After a number of complaints, a man from the company's New York office came and assured the women they had nothing to worry about.

Several women said they sent an anonymous letter to OSHA (Occupational Safety Health Administration), but all an OSHA inspector did was to order an eye bath for the women. It was not until the NRC came in that safety regulations became stricter.

One woman said calluses on her hands from yard work would glow in the dark after a shift at Luminous Processes. Rags used to clean contamination were kept in an open barrel. The women wore smocks to protect their clothes, but the smocks were cleaned only once a week. It was only in the last three months before the plant closed that the women were ordered to scrub their shoes before going home.

The practice of sending waste material to the city dump for burning was stopped by the Environmental Protection Agency (EPA). The material now had to be packed, sealed, and sent to a nuclear waste site.

My story in *The Daily Times* on April 26, 1978, told how Civil Defense Director (and former Ottawa mayor) Phil Bailey and I took a Geiger counter to the outside areas of the Luminous Processes building. We found levels that surprised Bailey because he did not expect that much on the outside of the building, especially since a janitor had washed down the steps and the outside of the building after it had closed. We could not get inside the locked building to take measurements.

It was the April 26 story that caused a public outrage in Ottawa—the biggest outcry since the Radium Dial hearings of the 1930s. The women told me the company did not tell them the plant was closing. The day the NRC suspended the license in February, the company told the women that "due to technical difficulties, do not report to work until next Wednesday." When the women called on Wednesday, after my first story was published, they were told to go to the unemployment office and apply for relief. They read in the newspaper the reason for closing the plant was high radiation levels. The newspaper stories may have been the reason that Luminous Processes officials did not respond to the NRC suspension and did not reopen its doors.

The company tried to move its machinery and equipment from the Ottawa building to its plant in Athens, Georgia, but the NRC stopped them because the equipment was too contaminated to be transported. The NRC also said the building was too contaminated for any other use. The company announced it would build a new plant in Huntsville, Alabama. However, it was not built.

The Ottawa women were left alone and did not even get the vacation and severance pay they were due. It was only after a number of newspaper stories that officials from Luminous Processes came to Ottawa. A public meeting was held in City Hall on May 1, 1978. The public packed the meeting room in City Hall.

The Luminous Processes officials were in a full defense mode, but that meeting did not go well for them. Warren Holmes, a technical manager for Luminous Processes in New York, denied that the building was a health hazard. He also denied that he was trying to "whitewash" the situation

The *Ottawa Daily Republican-Times* (later *The Daily Times*), with its unique glass block design, is pictured shortly after it was built in 1939.

in order to sell the building, although he admitted he was concerned about being able to sell it. He blamed the workers as much as the managers for any contamination inside the building.

Mr. Holmes claimed the violation of the license was the result of a "measuring problem." He said the technique used to measure radiation was different from the way it was measured when the company was first granted a license. If you could measure worm particles in tomato juice like you can measure radiation particles in the air, he said, you would never want to drink tomato juice again.

Also at the meeting were Alan Benckendorf, the former Ottawa plant manager who was moved to the Georgia plant, and Dr. Andrew Stehney from Argonne National Laboratory near Chicago. Dr. Stehney said it was his opinion that the chances for the Luminous Processes workers to get cancer was no higher than for workers anywhere else, but he added that research was not certain about that.

Dr. Stehney said Argonne began following Radium Dial and Luminous Processes workers, and he said about forty deaths could be linked to radium poisoning.

However, he insisted that he could not tell which tumors were caused by radiation and which were not. And he would not say categorically that the tumors were not caused by radioactive exposure at Luminous Processes.

When I asked Dr. Stehney if he would let his wife or daughter work at Luminous Processes, he said he would have reservations about that.

The Ottawa women had tough questions for the Luminous Processes spokesmen, and they were not satisfied by the answers. Mr. Holmes said tritium "tends to get all over the place, and spread and settle on surfaces." The women asked him why there were no exhaust fans in the building, since the material is harmful if inhaled or ingested. Mr. Holmes replied that the building did not lend itself to modern ventilation.

Luminous Processes building in 1978.

When Mr. Holmes said the company had "normal insurance" for workers, one woman asked if the company would pay medical claims if any ailments were discovered in the future. Mr. Holmes said no. Also, when several women asked, "Why weren't we told the truth about health hazards?" Mr. Holmes replied, "Communication could have been better."

One woman at the meeting said she had headaches from working there, and when she asked Mr. Benckendorf if she could work on a different machine, he refused. She was taken off the machine when her urine test showed a considerably higher radiation count than allowed. She said Mr. Benckendorf told her she should have stayed on that machine so they could see what effect it would have on her. "This is my life!" she exclaimed to the crowd at the meeting. "I don't want to be a guinea pig! They were taking a lot of chances without knowing what they were doing!" Mr. Benckendorf did not respond.

Mr. Benckendorf was asked if the layoff was permanent. He said "probably," and then admitted he knew a year earlier that the Ottawa facility probably was going to close.

After the two-and-a-half-hour meeting, the women said the company presentation was "a bunch of malarkey" and that Mr. Holmes was insensitive to their condition. They accused Luminous Processes of trying to "sneak out of town. All you want is to just get out and close the doors," one woman said. The editorial I wrote on May 4, 1978, summed up the meeting and the feelings of the women, concluding, "Luminous Processes seems to put profits before people. That may be the worst illness of all."

The day after the meeting, city officials contacted state and federal officials about the problem. The May 1 meeting, set up by Luminous Processes spokesmen, did not invite anyone from the Nuclear Regulatory Commission or the Illinois Department of Public Health (IDPH). Mayor James Thomas said the city would demolish the building if it was a health hazard.

Luminous Processes was required to make a survey of the extent of the radiation contamination. It said it would hire a New York company to do it. NRC spokesman Jan Strasma said he did not have confidence that Luminous Processes would do it right because "we've had a problem with Luminous in the past. They haven't had the equipment or the expertise to make an adequate survey."

Argonne National Laboratory was established in 1946. Studying the effects of radioactivity in human beings was one of its main functions. It began studying Ottawa dial painters in 1956.

——Commentary——

Doubletalk from Luminous

By JIM RIDINGS
Staff writer

Spokesmen from Luminous Processes spoke to former plant workers, the mayor, civil defense director and the press Monday to calm public fears that their building in Ottawa presented no great radiation hazard.

The company had a two-fold purpose: to convince potential buyers of the property that the building was safe and to discourage any possible lawsuits against the company from women workers who feel excessive radiation levels may be responsible for cancer they developed.

The company spokesmen should have stayed home.

The press was not convinced, the civil defense director was not convinced, and the women called the talk "a bunch of malarkey."

RIDINGS

Warren Holmes, company spokesman, gave the audience an education in doubletalk that would have made any national politician proud. He spouted irrelevant statistics about foreign countries, unfair comparisons about worms in tomato juice and deliberately gave technical data designed to confuse the women and the press in order not to be disputed.

Holmes also was so evasive when he played with semantics that he couldn't even say what was safe or dangerous because he said he couldn't define "safe" or "dangerous."

High radiation levels were not to be worried about, he said, because radiation is so easy to measure. If you could measure worm particles in tomato juice like you can measure radiation particles in the air, he said, you would never want to drink tomato juice again.

This is from a radiation chemist with 40 years experience, who apparently can't tell the health difference between ingesting worm particles and ingesting radioactivity.

Holmes said he didn't tell the women that tritium was "harmless"...he just said they "had nothing to worry about."

Holmes was asked why the building didn't have better ventilation...why the workers weren't told of the hazards...why radiation became so excessive the Nuclear Regulatory Commission was forced to shut the plant down. His only answers were a weak "We could have done more...there could have been better communication...everyone could have done a better job..."

Sorry that seven of ten women claim they developed breast cancer, he said, but anything could have caused that and you can't blame it on us.

Was the NRC right in closing the plant for violating their license? The NRC was right, said Holmes, "but not scientifically or technologically right." Right?

Holmes said safety measures weren't what they should be "because we didn't know the extent of the problem." The company has been doing this for 60 years, and should have learned something from the radium poisoning scandal of the 1920's and 1930's, when over a dozen Ottawa women died painfully from radium poisoning. A doctor from Argonne National Laboratories said Monday that since Argonne began monitoring Luminous women in the mid-1930's, over 40 deaths could be attributed to radiation from the plant. How many more women died from radiation that Argonne didn't catch?

For the women, the doubletalk is just beginning. They have to negotiate with Luminous for vacation and severance pay. When the plant closed in February, the women were promised $100 plus $5 for every year they worked at Luminous, a figure they called insulting. They have yet to see even that much, however.

Holmes came to Ottawa to present "factual knowledge rather than rumors and innuendos about the company as published in the newspaper." However, he admitted he had not read the newspaper story. When he did, he admitted he was "misinformed when the information was relayed," and "had a different impression" then. After reading the story, he agreed it was factual and correct.

The whole incident would be laughable if people's lives weren't at stake. Luminous Processes seems to put profits before people. It appears to take a casual attitude about safety precautions for its employees and has few regrets about any illnesses that may befall the workers.

That may be the worst illness of all.

The Daily Times, Ottawa, May 4, 1978.

Argonne exhumed the body of Margaret Looney from St. Columba Cemetery in Ottawa in 1978. Dr. Stehney told me that Argonne had been exhuming and studying bodies of radium victims across the country. Miss Looney was the first Ottawa victim to be exhumed.

Dr. Stehney said he was conducting a population study of women who worked with radium in the 1920s and was following the progress of radium workers who were still alive. He said he wanted to know where in the bones radium settled and how it distributed itself in the body.

He also said that not enough was known about radium in order to conclusively blame it for tumors suffered by the women at Luminous Processes, and that most doctors were reluctant to go on the record for lack of conclusive evidence. Argonne studied the bodies of victims for weeks before returning them to the cemetery. They did not make their findings public.

Another public meeting was held in Ottawa's City Hall on June 6, 1978. Representatives of the NRC and IDPH were present at this meeting. Bert Davis of the NRC said excessive radiation levels were found at the Luminous Processes building from the first NRC inspection in April 1976. Luminous continued to be in noncompliance in more inspections in 1976 and 1977. He said the company's license was suspended in February 1978 after the agency sent letters and met with company officials.

Maurice Neuweg, chief of the division of radiological health of the Illinois Department of Public Heath, said his agency found excessive radiation levels periodically since it began to monitor the building in 1957. Inspectors found bottles of radium paint in 1977, after Luminous Processes' license to have it expired. He said another inspection in May 1978, after the company closed, found more radium paint.

The state and federal spokesmen claimed the building posed no danger to the public. In October 1978, a team from the University of Georgia Center for Applied Isotope Studies came to Ottawa to survey the building and the homes of six female employees. The three-month study, released in May 1979, showed "considerable and substantial" amounts of radium and tritium contamination. The study showed tritium radiation in some parts of the Luminous Processes building at 1,666 times above NRC standards. Radium levels were hundreds of times higher than what is considered safe.

Where a dpm/100 cm level of 15,000 is the NRC limit, some areas of the building showed a level of 250,000 (dpm is a measure of radioactivity indicating the number of atoms in radioactive material that decays in one minute). Carl Paperiello, chief of materials and radiological protection for the NRC, said the measurements were taken from a smear of a 100-cm area, and that smear probably removed 1 percent of surface contamination—so an area measured at 250,000 dpm/100 cm could be as high as 25 million dpm-100cm.

Another study published by Dr. Stehney and others at Argonne National Laboratory in the fall of 1978 drew few conclusions about how radium affected recent Radium Dial workers, but it said that cancer deaths among workers was considerably higher than the general population.

The scientists studied 1,235 workers who began employment before 1930 at radium dial painting plants in Illinois, Connecticut, and New Jersey. The studies were conducted from the 1950s to the 1970s. It showed the average age of death was fifty-seven. A total of 529 deaths occurred before the age of eighty-five, where only 461 were expected. Fifty-eight died of bone sarcoma and eighteen died of head sarcoma, both cancers. The study pointed out its own flaw— the people measured were those who lived to be measured. The dozens of people who died in the 1920s and 1930s were not included, and the studies did not begin until the 1950s.

Another forty-one victims were measured after death, through autopsy or exhumation. The study remained inconclusive about deaths that were not directly attributed to bone cancer, citing variance in the amount of time an employee was exposed and the amount of radium which got into an employee. The study noted that "precautions taken in 1925 were adequate, for no radium-related malignancies have been observed in workers who entered this industry after 1925." However, it added that at the study's conclusion in 1976, "The cumulative survival of the population was significantly less than expected at ten or more years after first employment."

The report said its findings "indicate that only the known radium-related malignancies contributed significantly to life-shortening of the exposed population as a whole, but the presence of other radium-related causes of death may yet be detectable by examination of specific risks as a function of dose." It seems incredible that the study could be "inconclusive" given its own data.

Luminous Processes became a national news story, picked up by the wire services and printed in numerous newspapers across the country. The *Chicago Tribune* published a story on September 21, 1980. "If this is still the city of the walking dead, then I'm one of them," Pearl Schott told reporter Casey Bukro. "I'm a victim of cancer."

Tom Valeo wrote a great story in *The Sunday Herald Panorama* magazine, Arlington Heights, Illinois, on December 7, 1980. He wrote to me:

> Your articles gave me an excellent start. They were very well-researched and thorough, and pointed out things I never would have discovered on my own. You are very well-remembered in Ottawa, especially by the former dial painters. They never tire of telling me about the articles you did, and they all thought you were just wonderful.
>
> Some of the women complain of pain in their feet, one of the early symptoms of radium poisoning ... Some of the women have become anemic, a condition that develops when alpha particles from radium continuously bombard the bone marrow where blood cells are produced. And some have developed breast cancer and other tumors, diseases associated with exposure to ionizing radiation.

Anna Mayo of the *Village Voice* newspaper in Greenwich Village, New York, wrote a long story in December 1978. It began:

> They dug up Margaret Looney one day last spring. The exhumation took place in Ottawa, Illinois, pop. 20,000, one of those places New Yorkers think they've left behind. Mourners suddenly noticed that Looney's gravestone was missing, and it took Jim Ridings, a reporter for the Ottawa *Daily Times*, to locate it stored in the graveyard superintendent's shed.

Dr. Andrew Stehney told Miss Mayo that Argonne had examined about 2,000 people at that point. "Exhumation is not easy," he said. "Preparing the remains and all. Sometimes all we get is scraps. Maybe I shouldn't have said that."

"When a dial painter dies, a team from Argonne rushes to measure radium levels in the fresh corpse," Miss Mayo wrote.

Pearl Schott told Miss Mayo:

A man from the Luminous offices in New York was out here. He used to check on safety at the plant, and one time he asked me, "Pearl, how are you?" I said I had massive gastro-intestinal bleeding, and do you know what he told me? He said, "Don't worry about it, lots of people have that."

An unidentified woman told Miss Mayo:

One close friend of mine got a lump behind her ear and died three days after she entered the hospital. She was forty-three years old. I remember feeling that lump. She cried, "Oh, when I first went to Luminous I was so healthy! You wouldn't believe how healthy I was."

Anna Mayo asked Dr. Stehney, "When the women's doctors asked you for your opinion, I suppose that you told them that there was no evidence that radium exposure had anything to do with their illnesses?" Dr. Stehney replied, "That's right. There's no evidence." She asked, "Did you tell them there is no evidence that radium did not cause their illnesses?" He answered, "Why, no! I can't think of any reason to have told them that. Why would I have told them that?"

Ottawa mortician William Hulse told Miss Mayo that scientists from Argonne came to his funeral home more than a dozen times to examine the bodies of former radium workers.

The scientists come down here and they put the body up on lead blocks and they go to work with their Geiger counters. No, the bodies don't glow, but I suspect the skeletons do. No, there's no danger for me to handle the bodies. I'm not a robot in a lead suit or anything. But if you go down to the cemetery with a Geiger counter and hold it over the graves of those girls who died from radium poisoning, you can get it clacking, let me tell you.

10

THE LOCKER PLANT

A story in the May 24, 1978, *Daily Times,* by reporters Jim Ridings and Joan Hustis, questioned whether the high cancer rate in Ottawa was due to Radium Dial. Radium Dial was located in the former high school building from 1922 to 1937. Built as the township's high school in 1879 at a cost of $12,000, the city claimed it was the biggest high school building in the state outside of Chicago.

After Radium Dial left, the LaSalle County Farm Bureau and other agencies moved into the old building, including the Home Bureau, Ag Soil Conservation Association, Farm Bureau Soil Testing Service, Breeding Cooperative, Ottawa PCA, Ottawa National Farm Loan Association, Illinois State Employment Service, and the Ottawa Women's Club. Co-Operative Refrigerated Services operated a meat locker in the basement from 1940 to 1955. That was where radium had been stored. Farmers stored, packed, processed, and shipped meat from the building for fifteen years. Also, the large room where the dial painting had been done was used for Farm Bureau dinners and banquets for school and scout organizations, and food was prepared in the building.

The LaSalle County Farm Bureau moved to a new building on Route 23 north of Ottawa in 1968. The old building was never decontaminated because such an effort was never considered at the time.

Dr. Roger Linnemann, associate professor of radiology at the University of Pennsylvania, who was working on a study of workers at a nearby nuclear power plant in Morris, told the reporters that the degree of contamination of meat depended on the amount of radium lingering on walls and floors. No measurements were taken at the time the meat was stored there, and the building was gone in 1978.

Dr. Linnemann said it could take fifteen to thirty years for cancer to develop, depending on the extent of the exposure to an individual. Radium goes to the bone and sits there, Dr. Linnemann said. One of the directors of the meat locker corporation died of bone cancer in the mid-1970s.

The 1978 story cited LaSalle County's death rate from cancer at 232 deaths per 100,000 persons. The death rate in the United States was 171 per 100,000 and 186 per 100,000 in the state of Illinois at that time. Another study in 1997 by Northern Illinois University also showed an above average cancer rate in Ottawa.

Darlene Halm lived near the old building and remembered when it was torn down in 1969. "People would help themselves to souvenirs," she said. "This was before anyone knew the debris was contaminated. The demolition created a lot of dust. It would seep in the houses, and we would have to dust the furniture every day."

Ken Ricci, an environmental activist in Ottawa, noted that many people took bricks from the demolition site and built fireplaces, porches, and more, without realizing that the porous bricks absorbed radium. He has used his Geiger counter at places around town and has proven it.

Both of Darlene Halm's parents died of cancer, as did a number of other people who lived in that neighborhood, she said. Other relatives and neighbors who lived in Retz's subdivision on Ottawa's northeast side died of rare cancers, Darlene said. That area is located at the bottom of a steep hill from St. Columba and Oakwood cemeteries. Darlene said she wonders if rainwater went downhill from the cemeteries to the wells in that neighborhood.

Some of the debris from the Radium Dial demolition was used to fill in the basement, before the lot was blacktopped. The majority of the debris was hauled and dumped to a number of sites around Ottawa. Decades later, millions of Superfund dollars would be spent to clean up the hazardous material.

Ottawa's high school building before it was occupied by Radium Dial, when the building still had a steeple.

The last hot spot is at the junction of Routes 6 and 71. Not only was rubble dumped there in 1969, that site had been a city dump for decades, with Radium Dial dumping its waste material over many years. Mr. Ricci said his Geiger counter's needle went off the chart when he went there. It still was registering at the top as far as 15 feet about the ground.

Tamara Craig of Ottawa said that her grandfather, Henry Hoenes, was the superintendent of Brickton Bricks. He was asked by the manager of Radium Dial in 1937, after it closed, to take two containers of radium and bury them in the clay hills along Routes 6 and 71. Her grandmother, Adeline (Johnson) Hoenes, worked at Radium Dial and was among the women who were later studied by Argonne National Laboratory.

After Radium Dial closed in December 1936, it donated its highly contaminated desks to St. Francis Catholic Grade School in Ottawa. In 1980, more than four decades later, the state removed them because they still gave off contamination levels ten times above the acceptable level.

The Farm Bureau sold the old Radium Dial building to Ben Schwartz of Marshalltown, Iowa. Schwartz paid local contractor Martin Serena to tear it down. Schwartz, who owned six Burger Chef franchises in Iowa, was planning on opening one in Ottawa. He changed his mind and sold the land in 1972 to Donald Pool for a used car lot. When I spoke to a Burger Chef company spokesman in 1978, he said the company did not keep a file on why a site was rejected, but a decision could be affected by what was previously located on the site. That corner remained a vacant lot for fifty years—until the asphalt was removed and excavation was done for a new Subway sandwich shop in 2019.

11

CLEANUP TIME

Illinois Attorney General Tyrone Fahner asked for a restraining order in September 1980 to prevent Luminous Processes from removing machines and material that might be radioactive from its building. Mr. Fahner also asked that Luminous build a fence around its property and post a security guard. Mr. Fahner said the company abandoned its building, and that vandals broke windows, exposing the public to radiation.

Mr. Fahner's document—which named both the company and its president, Joseph Kelly, Jr.—added an affidavit from George McCann, a health physicist with the Illinois Department of Public Health, saying that the building contained radiation twelve times greater that public health standards. Mr. Fahner estimated the cost to clean up the Ottawa site would be $500,000. It ended up being many times more than that. Mr. Kelly claimed his company did not have the money for the cleanup, and he said he would decontaminate their Georgia Plant before he started in Ottawa.

Judge Frank Yackley issued the restraining order on September 17, 1980. He did not grant the request for a fence or a guard, but he did order the windows to be boarded and signs to be posted warning of radioactivity. Judge Yackley ruled in December 1980 that Luminous had to clean up the building by the following March 15. Nothing was done, so Judge Leonard Hoffman ordered it again on June 24. Joseph Kelly, Jr., then claimed the company had no money to decontaminate the Ottawa building or its building in Athens, Georgia. The Georgia plant operated from 1952 to 1978. The company abandoned the Georgia plant in 1980.

The state of Georgia said the Luminous Processes plant there was its worst hazardous site. A state environmental official said Luminous Processes "had gone out back and just dug holes and buried old watch dials and watch hands and everything else. We had to remove up to five feet or six feet of dirt around the building just to get rid of the stuff." U.S. Superfund money was used in 1982 to clean up the Athens plant, amounting to $800,000. Kelly paid nothing.

Radiation was found to be leaking from the Ottawa building in July 1981. Someone spray-painted the 60-foot side of the Ottawa building, "DIAL LUMINOUS FOR DEATH." Decontamination began in April 1983, by a company from Cayce, South Carolina. Contaminated soil outside the building was removed by state and city workers. The dirt was placed in about three dozen drums and

"Dial Luminous For Death."

shipped to a nuclear waste dump in Hanford, Washington. Bricks were sent to a landfill in nearby Pontiac. Demolition was finished in late 1985. Excavation of contaminated soil beneath the building was done in 1986. However, much more work was needed.

A trial date was set for July 1983 to prove Radium Chemical Company was liable for the cost of cleanup. Instead, an agreement was reached in which Radium Chemical agreed to conditions in the cleanup. Once again, they skipped out.

State Representative Peg Breslin of Ottawa asked the state legislature in May 1983 for $2 million to clean up the plant. Her bill passed and was signed by Governor James Thompson in January 1984. Another $1.5 million was needed, and was approved, in July 1985.

The Luminous project set new standards for removing contaminated material. Mike Parker, project director of the state's department of nuclear safety, told the local newspaper that the department had never undertaken management of such a large project. Precautions that never before had been used were being taken, and it would be a blueprint for future work.

The entire matter of the Luminous Processes scandal uncovered four "hot spots" in Ottawa in 1985 that were also contaminated by radium: a parking lot behind the Veterans of Foreign War building at 1016 Columbus Street; a vacant lot on Lafayette Street near the Marquette High School track; an empty field behind Dougherty Manor at Post Street and the Fox River; and a field behind Midwest Landscaping at Routes 6 and 71. These, and other locations, were sites where debris from the Radium Dial plant was dumped in 1969.

Martin Serena, the contractor who demolished the old Radium Dial building, said he dumped the rubble at two places: a field north of Floyd Cavanaugh's home on Porter Road, on land that was owned by Bob Herman, at the base of the North Bluff clay hills; and in a 50-foot gully south of the Hilltop Tavern on Rural Route 1. Most of the debris went in a gully behind the Hilltop, which owners Pasquale Vignochi and Jeno Monteraselli wanted filled in so they could build a parking lot on the site. The rubble that went near the North Bluff area went to fill in a swamp.

Mr. Serena gave the top notch from a main staircase newel post to the high school superintendent. It was kept in his office as a memento of the old building.

Radon was found in numerous Ottawa houses in 1986. Radon is an odorless gas linked to cancers. One house had the highest level of radon gas found in the state, twenty-five times higher than a level considered safe. The address was not disclosed, but the state said the one-story, white clapboard house on the northeast side of Ottawa was built on land that had been filled with rubble from the Radium Dial building. The state spent $60,000 to clean up the house.

Dial faces and hands at Luminous Processes.

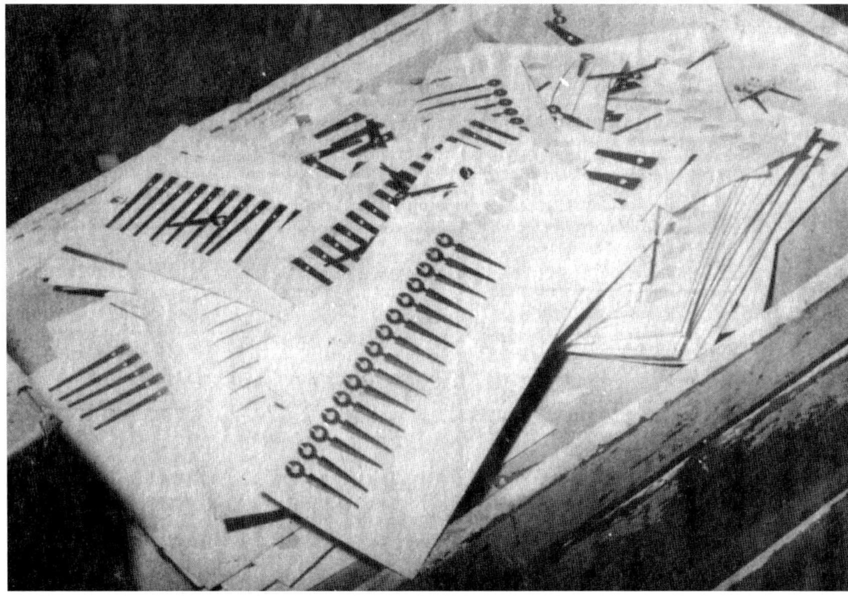

By 1994, the United States EPA had identified nineteen "hot spots" in Ottawa and allocated $18.5 million to clean them up, the most money the EPA had spent on a Superfund site at that time. By the end of 1995, work was halted when the fund ran out of money after cleaning up ten sites and spending $28 million. Work resumed in 2006, when more Superfund money was available.

Soil samples at a depth of 6 inches near homes and businesses by the Luminous Processes site in July 1985 found radiation levels fifty-two times higher than levels considered safe.

The Daily Times reported in 1988 that radioactive items were turning up around Ottawa. A garage and a barbecue grill made of bricks form the Luminous Processes site were torn down. Eighty bottles used in the factory were found in a local business. The caps on the bottles and the bricks were highly radioactive and were taken to a nuclear dump.

A vial of radium was found in a warehouse on Chestnut Street in 1989, a site that was designated a hot spot. Two vials containing a total of 1 millicurie of radium were found in a house at 923 Sycamore Street in 1995. They were left there by a former owner, Lester Mettille, who had been a janitor at Luminous Processes. He sold the house in 1975. The vials were discovered by crews surveying the alley, which was one of the hot spots. They could detect the radium from the outside, in one wall and in the attic of the house. The elderly couple who owned the house in 1995 did not express concern.

12

WHERE ARE THE LUMINOUS OWNERS?

The Luminous Processes owners went into hiding. They dissolved the company in the early 1980s and transferred the assets to a subsidiary company, Radium Chemical Incorporated. All were headquartered in Manhattan, New York. Joseph Kelly, Jr., was in charge.

The state of Illinois filed a lien on the Luminous Processes property in November 1986. The state wanted the property owners to pay some of the $4.5 million that was spent on the cleanup. "Officials say, however, say locating Luminous Processes officials and getting the money is akin to squeezing blood from a turnip," *The Daily Times* reported. On top of that, the property was mortgaged, so any money from the sale of the land would first go to the lender, Streator Home Building and Loan Association. Back taxes also were owed. Disposition of the vacant property was settled in 1988. Streator Home Building and Loan Association gave up trying to collect its $13,955 mortgage because it knew collection from Radium Chemical was hopeless.

A crew from CBS Channel 2 in Chicago came to Ottawa in September 1983 to do a story. They interviewed Norman Hulse, a local undertaker. Mr. Hulse told Channel 2 that he embalmed the bodies of a dozen Radium Dial women from the 1930s. Most of the radium the women ingested settled in the pelvic region after their kidneys filtered it from their blood, he said. Mr. Hulse told the reporter that fifty years later, his Geiger counter still detected radiation coming from the graves of the victims. It was the smaller, thinner women who got sick first. The death certificates gave leukemia as the cause of death. "It was an easy out," Hulse said.

Carole Langer, a documentary filmmaker from New York, made a film in 1987 about the Radium Dial story. *Radium City* made its premier at the American Film Institute Festival of Independent Films at the Kennedy Center in New York in November 1987. The 102-minute film told the story of Radium Dial and Luminous Processes, and the stories of several women who worked there, including Marie Rossiter.

Mrs. Rossiter was one of the first people Miss Langer met when she came to Ottawa. She asked Mrs. Rossiter why, when so many other dial painters had died, was she still alive? Mrs. Rossiter replied, "God left me here so someday someone would walk through the door and I would be able to tell them the truth."

Marie Rossiter and Carole Langer in 1987. On the left is Marie's son, William Rossiter.

It was the spark that led Carole Langer on her four-year task on the film. "These victims cry out from their graves for justice," Miss Langer said. Carole Langer did not start out to make a film about the Ottawa radium workers. Her intent was to make a film about women who took dangerous jobs because they desperately needed the money. When she got to Ottawa, she changed her focus to radium workers.

The film was shown in Ottawa on February 9, 1988, to two standing-room-only crowds. It was shown in the Glass Worker's Union Hall because local theaters would not screen it. The film was condemned by Mayor George Small, who refused an invitation to the screening because he said it gave the city a black eye.

"If people want to see it, that's their business," Mayor Small told *The Daily Times*. "But I don't intend to promote a movie made by someone from New York that makes our community look bad. Let her stay in New York and make a movie there."

A local activist group, Residents Against a Polluted Environment, was formed. It successfully fought a proposed hazardous waste landfill, a proposed incinerator, it joined in the effort to get the Luminous Processes site cleaned up, and it helped to get the state and federal governments to clean up the radioactive hot spots around Ottawa.

Among these activists who made LaSalle County a better place were Robert Eschbach (who later served as mayor of Ottawa), Ken Ricci, Katie (Dumke) Troccoli, Ogden Andrews, Ario Franzetti, Bennett Bray, Daphne Mitchell, Mary Lou Mitchell, Larry and Joan Bernabie, Deb Parisot, Ted Parisot, Gert Barron, Mike Barron, Brent Barron, Scott Stewart, Mike Bosanovich, Sharon

Fordon, Bruce Markwalter, Barry Sanders, Bill Rosencranz, Lois Sampson, Joe Karaganis, Nick Maningacina, Harry Jacobs, Janet Kammer Kiesig, Bob and Marylea Dumke, Alexander Troccoli, Krisy Troccoli, Jen Troccoli Farrell, Lenny Newell, Karin Oslanzi Kummer, and Lance Yednock.

Despite the distinguished individuals who spearheaded the effort to clean up Ottawa, they found stiff opposition from the local powers. Katie Troccoli said:

> We went to Ottawa City Hall to bring it to their attention that there was a radioactive problem in River City ... Mayor Thomas called me a little school girl. He said, "Why, I'd eat lunch in that building," to which I replied, "I'm buying, but you're eating alone."
>
> They had sheriff's deputies and city police in attendance at that City Council meeting, in case we got violent. We had no intention of ever being violent.

Mrs. Troccoli was working at Wheeler Realty at the time. Fred Wheeler, the broker, received a phone call warning him to fire Mrs. Troccoli. She said:

> I was his top producer, and he kept me ... He was genuinely concerned for my well-being.
>
> You have to remember we were also fighting the hazardous waste landfill west of town. We were organizing in Marseilles to fight a mega landfill, at Sheridan to stop a hazardous waste incinerator, and in Oglesby to stop Illinois Cement from burning hazardous waste in the cement kiln.
>
> Prior to that I worked for Carol Seward. I ran for City Council. Boy, was I naive. Her husband Harry worked at the plastic plant between Ottawa and Marseilles. He put my bumper sticker on his truck. He was told by management to remove the sticker or lose his job.
>
> My Dad was a World War II 82nd Airborne paratrooper. He taught me to speak up for those who can't speak up for themselves. He made three combat jumps, fought in the Battle of the Bulge and helped liberate Wobbelin Concentration Camp in Ludwigslust, Germany. If I had a bad day at school and complained, he would show me pictures of the concentration camp in the book, *Saga of the All American*. You can't grow up with that and be quiet to injustice.

As preparations were made for demolition of the Luminous Processes building, former worker Martha Hartshorn was among those who toured the building in March 1984.

It is curious how the government found where the biggest hot spots were.

When the EPA asked Martin Serena where he had dumped the building debris from Radium Dial, he pretended he did not know. However, he was on videotape in footage that had been cut from Miss Langer's documentary. Residents Against a Polluted Environment had that footage and let EPA investigators Vernetta Simon and Bill Reynolds see it. They went back to Mr. Serena, and he had to admit that he knew what was hauled and where it was dumped.

The demolition and removal of the Luminous Processes building began in 1984. The building was in the downtown business district. Ken Ricci watched the demolition of the building in 1985. He said there were four primary workers, and they seemed to carelessly handle material. They would cut boards, with sawdust flying everywhere. Then they would sit down and eat lunch. Dust was hosed down, into the city sewers. Mr. Ricci said those four men died of cancer within a few years. They went to Argonne to be studied, but the results were not released.

Mike Kohr worked as a delivery man for United Parcel Service in 1984:

> I would deliver Next Day Air envelopes from the EPA in Washington D.C. to the hermetically sealed headquarters trailer at the site of the on-going demolition of the Luminous Processes building. The guy in the trailer usually had booties over his feet, and a white pull-on work suit. One day, I noted his safety outfit and the super-sealed trailer he worked out of, and I questioned why the laborers that were taking the building down were dressed in regular work clothes. He just gave me a sheepish look and shrugged his shoulders.

Joseph A. Kelly, Jr., signed a nine-page agreement with the state of New York in October 1987 to accept full legal responsibility for decontaminating its property in Queens. The agreement called for Mr. Kelly to pay up to $500,000 of the cost, even though the cost was estimated at $6 million. Mr. Kelly signed the agreement to avoid prosecution. A *New York Times* article said Kelly's building was emitting gamma radiation forty times above permissible levels, and radium contamination was found in a nearby sewer.

The Orange, New Jersey, location was cleaned by U.S. EPA Superfund money. Kelly once again got away. Cleanup of the sixteen sites in Ottawa designated for federal EPA Superfund money is still being done in 2020.

Fences and scaffolding went up in May 1985 around the Luminous Processes building.

Workers wore protective clothing when they started dismantling the Luminous Processes building in August 1985.

13

DENIAL

From the very beginning, Radium Dial spokesmen lied and denied—they lied to the women about the danger of radium; they lied to the women about their results of their physical exams; they paid Ottawa doctors to lie on the death certificates; they paid Ottawa lawyers to refuse to take the women's cases; they refused to cooperate with government health inspectors; and they denied any responsibility for the dozens of their women who were dying the most agonizing deaths.

In fighting the case of Inez Vallat, company lawyers argued that radium was a poison, and since poison was not covered by the law, the case had no merit. When the law was changed to include poisons, the company lawyers argued (in Catherine Donohue's case) that the radium paint was not poisonous, so the lawsuit had no merit.

Radium Dial officials argued that radium paint did not cause radium poisoning, and then argued that the women who were dying from radium poisoning were not entitled to compensation because they were no longer employees. In an appeal of the Donohue verdict, Radium Dial lied by denying that anyone told the women that radium would not hurt them. They lied by denying they told the women to tip the brushes in their mouths, and they lied when they opened Luminous Processes and said dial painting there was safe.

The same was true for the radium workers in New Jersey and Connecticut. The company doctors and spokesmen denied that the cancers, the teeth falling out, and the jaws disintegrating were caused by radium poisoning. They denied it, even when their own chemists were dying.

It is unbelievable that doctors in Ottawa and New Jersey could see similar, odd symptoms such as teeth and jaws falling apart and strange cancers and not realize that the common thread was that all the patients worked with radium, a known deadly compound.

Mary Doty of the *Chicago Times* wrote in 1936 about seeing women on the streets of Ottawa, some barely able to walk, others with "an empty coat sleeve or a mutilated nose, withered hands, a shrunken jaw." The doctors, lawyers, and everyone else also could see this, conditions exclusive to the women of Radium Dial, and they still denied the obvious. The death certificates of the women in New Jersey, Connecticut, and Ottawa listed the cause of death as diphtheria, anemia, syphilis, pneumonia, and more—anything but radium poisoning.

It most certainly was known at that time that radium exposure killed people; Dr. Harrison Martland proved it in 1925. George Willis, who started a dial painting company in 1914 with Sabin von Sochocky, wrote in 1923, "There is good reason to fear that neglect of precautions may result in serious injury to the radium workers themselves." When von Sochocky, died of radium poisoning in 1928, *The New York Times* headlined his death, "Radium Paint Takes Its Inventor's Life. Poisoned by Watch Dial Luminant."

Radium Dial was unable to get liability insurance after 1928 because of all the lawsuits from its victims. Joseph A. Kelly played the victim, complaining to the Illinois Industrial Commission about how liability could threaten his company. He cared more about the profitability and health of his company than the health of the women who made his company profitable, oblivious to the outrageous arrogance and irony of his words. Kelly, in a letter to New York's commissioner of Public Health dated June 18, 1928, acknowledged the illnesses, while turning on the women he was killing:

> The dial painting work was easy, the operators well paid, and as conditions turned out, we unfortunately gave work to a great many people who were physically unfit to procure employment in other lines of industry. Cripples and persons similarly incapacitated were engaged. What was then considered an act of kindness on our part has since been turned against us, as all previous employees, regardless of what they may have been suffering from or are suffering from at the present time, in the minds of the general public can be attributed to "Radium Poisoning."
>
> In the early part of 1924, it was called to our attention, through a highly reputable dental firm, that some of our employees were suffering from what was believed to be phosphorus poisoning. There was a thought at the time that if a condition existed it might be due to the brushes, and therefore all brushes were thoroughly sterilized before being used by the operators. Absolute instructions were given not to point the brushes with the lips. We also engaged Dr. Cecil K. Drinker of the Industrial Hygiene Section of the Harvard School of Medicine to make a survey of our plant and to make recommendations. Dr. Drinker made several trips to the plant, made numerous tests, and finally reported on June 3, 1924, that since he could find no direct cause for the apparent trouble which existed, radium looked suspicious.
>
> In the early part of 1925, two suits were instituted against the corporation, claiming injury from their employment. About this time the Consumer's League of New Jersey took an active interest in the matter, and enlisted the support of Dr. Frederick L. Hoffman, statistician for the Prudential Insurance Company. Although not a physician and having no knowledge regarding radium, Dr. Hoffman read a paper before the American Medical Association Convention in Atlantic City, May 1925, and named the disease in New Jersey "Radium Necrosis." Dr. Hoffman claims credit for having discovered this so-called disease, and we believe the published literature bears out his contention.
>
> Confronted with lawsuits, and with a paper purporting to have discovered a brand new disease among our former employees, also propaganda from the Consumer's League of New Jersey, we took further advice from competent medical authorities on what should be done. It was suggested that the Industrial Hygiene section of the College of Physicians and Surgeons, Columbia University, might undertake scientific investigations to ascertain if there really was danger existing in the industry. Dr. Frederick B. Flinn became interested in March 1925,

and began a scientific study of the question. Based on the scientific data acquired, which was undoubtedly the most thorough study of the subject, Dr. Flinn reached the conclusion that there was no industrial hazard in the industry.

However, soon after this article appeared there was brought to his attention a case of a former applicator who contained a certain amount of radioactivity. While there were other implications involved, after a period of 6 or 8 months observation and treatment, and a final autopsy, Dr. Flinn reached the conclusion that undoubtedly radioactivity contributed to the condition of the girl.

Perhaps it would not be amiss to discuss briefly the recent suits against this corporation, which have received so much unwarranted and untrue publicity. Through a, no doubt, cleverly designed campaign of publicity, the public was appealed to and the appeal met a responsive chord. The spectacle of five women filled with radium, doomed to a speedy and terrible death, according to experts, presented a gruesome picture indeed. The fact that we settled these suits in no way is indicative of the merits of the complainants' contentions, or that we admit responsibility or liability. From a legal aspect there is very little question but that we had a perfect defense, both from the standpoint of the Statute of Limitations and from the fact that there was no negligence on our part.

Robert Rowland of Argonne National Laboratory commented in 1994 on Kelly's letter:

Interestingly, this letter did not mention the findings and the many publications of Dr. H. S. Martland, who firmly and without hesitation stated that the problems in the industry were due to radium and mesothorium.

Radium Dial spent the money to hire a fake doctor to examine their workers in New Jersey and tell them they were all right, even though they were glowing with radioactivity, but it did not spend the money to compensate the dying women.

The dial painters found it difficult to find lawyers, and when they did, the company used delays in court, hoping the women would die before their cases came to trial.

Catherine Donahue testified in 1938 that she began having trouble with her teeth, legs, and hip after working at Radium Dial for a few years. Doctors acknowledged the problems were real, but they would not blame radium poisoning. When her limping became evident, she was fired in order not to alarm the other women of the problem. Even when her jawbone started falling out in pieces, Ottawa doctors refused to point to radium poisoning. When she sought compensation, the company fought her every inch of the way, all the way to her early death and beyond.

Dr. Charles Loeffler of Chicago examined Mrs. Donohue and told company officials that they should examine their workers for radium poisoning. The company refused.

Radium Dial was so obstructive that it would not cooperate with the U.S. Department of Labor's inquiry into the radium deaths. When the government asked about Margaret Looney, the company would only say that she was still employed, even though she had died several months earlier. It also objected to the name "radium poisoning," even though Margaret had tested positive for radium in 1928 and she had been told by Chicago doctors to change her employment. In a brief in the Donohue case, attorney Leonard Grossman wrote:

> I cannot imagine a fiend fresh from the profoundest depths of perdition committing such an unnatural crime as the Radium Dial Company did. My God, is the radium industry utterly destitute of shame? Is the Radium Dial Company utterly dominated by a beast? It is an offense against morals and humanity. And, incidentally, against the law.

Inez Vallat died in 1936, bleeding to death from a cancerous tumor in her neck, a wound too great for the doctors to stop the bleeding. The Ottawa doctors said on the death certificate that the cause of death was not work-related. The doctors repeated that as victim after victim died of radium poisoning.

In a story on July 7, 1939, *Chicago Times* writer John Main noted that no Ottawa lawyer would take the case of the victims. "Ottawa bitterly resented, resents to this day, these poor women's charges as giving a 'black eye' to the community." In fact, it was Ottawa lawyer Andrew J. O'Conor who successfully represented Radium Dial against these women in the cases that ended with the state's occupational diseases law being thrown out.

After Mr. Cook withdrew in 1937 as the lawyer for the Ottawa women, William Ganley, spokesman for Radium Dial in Ottawa, told the *Chicago Times*:

> These women's claims are invalid and illegitimate. We beat several suits in the lower courts in Illinois, and the verdicts in our favor were upheld by the state Supreme Court. We don't feel any legitimate claims have been filed against us. A lot of those women were with us only a few months and never did any direct work with the radioactive salts we use in our process. Practically all of them have been out of our employ for many years. I can't recall a single actual victim of this so-called radium poisoning in our Ottawa plant.

When any worker began to show symptoms of radium poisoning, it was the company's policy to fire the woman so that other workers wouldn't notice her. Catherine Donahue testified to that in 1938. Even the federal government was in denial about radiation from atomic tests. The Atomic Energy Commission stated the risks were worth it in order to stay ahead of our enemies in nuclear weapons.

In Ottawa, a spokesman for the Nuclear Regulatory Commission downplayed the hazard of tritium, after the NRC suspended Luminous Processes' license in February 1978 for having unsafe radiation levels in the building. Jan Strasma told me, "Adequate precautions are needed in handling of tritium, and while misuse could affect one's health, tritium is not the hazard radium is."

It seems odd that the plant was shut down because of the excessive levels of tritium, while a spokesman was downplaying the hazards of tritium.

"Any form of radiation can cause cancer," Mr. Strasma added. "Properly handled, it should not be a hazard to employees." Mr. Strasma's statement may or may not be accurate, but it is irrelevant when the material is not properly handled and when the managers do not take adequate precautions.

The company started taking weekly urine samples from the women, which showed "measurable but not hazardous" levels of tritium, Strasma said. So why did so many women who worked at Luminous Processes develop breast cancer and other cancers? Mr. Strasma said he thought the illnesses may have been caused by radium exposure over previous years. At a public meeting in 1978, company spokesman Warren Holmes blamed the workers for contamination.

Argonne had been exhuming and studying bodies of radium victims across the country, including Ottawa victims. Even after all their study, Dr. Andrew Stehney said that "not enough was known about radium in order to conclusively blame it for tumors suffered by the women at Luminous Processes, and that most doctors were reluctant to go on the record for lack of conclusive evidence."

I asked Luminous Processes workers in 1978 if they thought the radium and tritium caused their ailments. "In our minds, we feel it did," one woman told me. "But our doctors do not want to take a chance and come out and say it."

In the matter of how radium may have contaminated meat in the former Radium Dial building, Dr. Roger Linnemann said in 1978 that it was difficult to tie any cancers to radioactive meat. He said there are so many cancer-causing agents, so it is difficult to tie a cancer to one cause. "But I wouldn't open a meat locker where radium had been stored," he told me in an interview. "Absolutely not. I'd tell you you're out of your mind."

A statement by an Argonne spokesman that perhaps forty deaths could be attributed to radium poisoning was ludicrous. Argonne examined thousands of workers, many after their deaths, and found radium poisoning in hundreds of victims. Their study's claim that "no radium-related malignancies have been observed in workers who entered this industry after 1925" is beyond ludicrous.

Robert Rowland, director of Argonne's Center for Human Radiobiology, told a UPI reporter that any meat stored in the plant would not have absorbed enough radiation to be hazardous. However, he added, any radiation in a piece of meat would have to be 100 times more than the radiation in a watch dial. Women who worked there said radium was handled carelessly and sometimes was spilled. That certainly would have met the higher level.

The denial began in the 1920s and continued for decades. Mayors James Thomas (who served from 1967 to 1987), George Small (1987 to 1991), and Forrest Buck (1991 to 1999) all had unfavorable views of the publicity because they thought it gave the city a bad name.

In a story in the *Chicago Tribune* on January 30, 1984, Mayor Thomas told reporter R. Bruce Dold, "I'm not that scared of that building. It wouldn't bother me one bit to go in and sit down inside that building. It's nothing much, just an eyesore.... Many people think it's a shame that $2 million is being spent on this building. There are a lot of other ways to spend it." City Hall was less than two blocks from the building. The mayor said his wife and sister had been dial painters.

"The battle over Luminous Processes has created deep divisions in this town of 18,700 people," Dold wrote. "Many question the seriousness of the problem and whether activists who lobbied for the clean-up should not have left well enough alone."

Mayor Thomas told an Associated Press reporter in 1998, "I've never been too thrilled about all the publicity that's been handed out about this over the years. Most folks in town would like to put that thing to rest. They'd just like to get on with their lives."

It was, according to Darlene Halm, "a big cover-up. They just wanted the whole thing done with."

The Daily Times, which had given me a free hand to report and to write commentaries in 1978 and 1979, had new editors in 1984 when it published a front-page editorial on March 30. Chicago TV stations came to town to cover the upcoming demolition of the Luminous Processes building, and the editors took offense when the reporters called Ottawa "Death City." The editorial began, "They are like locusts. They don't crave grain but live on a diet of sensation, washed down by inaccuracy. They are the major media, which have suddenly discovered in part a 60-year old story." It called the story of radium deaths "ancient hat" with several inaccuracies. The editorial had its own inaccuracies, saying, "The women died allegedly of radium poisoning," and the deaths were Radium Dial workers, not Luminous Processes workers (it was both). It even objected that a TV station ran the story of the cleanup in Ottawa after a story about a murder.

Argonne National Laboratory opened a Center for Human Radiobiology to study the dial painters, both deceased and still working, to determine how much radioactivity they had and what might be an unsafe level. This started in the 1960s and continued until the program ran out of money in the 1990s. The women were examined and put through a series of tests, many coming back numerous times over the years. However, the women were never told the results of the tests. The women were led to believe that these exams might lead to stopping cancers or deaths caused by their exposure in the workplace.

Charlotte Purcell was persuaded by Argonne scientists to have an operation on her hip in the 1970s. She was never told anything more than "small amounts of radium" were found. Mrs. Purcell underwent numerous X-rays exams before finally refusing in 1985 to cooperate any further. The lack of information from Argonne led many other dial painters to discontinue returning for more examinations. Lloyd Vallat refused to let Argonne exhume his wife's remains in 1984.

Refusals by Argonne to disclose information, even to the subjects they examined, was seen as part of the denial. However, in recent years, Argonne has been willing to finally admit that their studies confirmed that the victims died of radium poisoning, not other diseases listed by doctors on death certificates.

14

ACCEPTANCE

The city's official resistance finally ended when Robert Eschbach became mayor of Ottawa in 1999. Mr. Eschbach was part of the citizen's movement that sought to identify and clean up the radioactive hot spots in Ottawa. He helped end the denial of the obvious that Ottawa had taken for more than sixty years.

The citizens and the city officials today have a different attitude toward this story than they did in 1936, 1938, 1978 or 1988, when the scandal hit its high points. Instead of criticizing writers and filmmakers who told the story, and instead of claiming that a moniker of "Radium City" gives the city a bad name, it is generally accepted that this is a part of history that needs to be acknowledged.

A monument to the "Radium Girls" is on the site where Luminous Processes stood for more than fifty years. A story board is near the statue, telling visitors the history of the event. The memorial came about after members of the Mendota History Club, in a town just north of Ottawa, wrote and produced a play, *Radium Girls*, in 2006. It earned them national recognition at the National History Day competition in Washington, D.C.

One of the schoolgirls, thirteen-year-old Madeline Pillar, decided that there should be a monument to the local women who died in this tragedy. She asked the Ottawa City Council for its support. She met with Mayor Eschbach, who liked her idea. It was decided the memorial should be on the Luminous Processes site, which the city then owned.

Mayor Eschbach sent a letter on city stationary to Madeline on July 30, 2010. He pledged the city's "strong support" and said:

The tragic and courageous story of the Radium Girls is an important part of the history of the City of Ottawa which deserves to be recognized and remembered by the citizens of Ottawa. It also is a story which needs to be shared with those who visit Ottawa. I believe the development of a beautiful and moving memorial such as the planned life-sized original bronze artwork dedicated to these young women will appropriately fulfill this important need.

The Radium Girl statue, on the site where the Luminous Processes building once stood at 801 Clinton Street in Ottawa. A paint brush is in one hand, a rose is in the other hand.

Next page: The plaza with the Radium Girl statue, waterfall, and story boards.

The mayor said the city would donate the land, design and prepare the site, provide landscaping, provide signs and plaques, and aid with the finances.

Madeline and others, including her father, William, who is a sculptor, began a fund-raising drive. Local labor unions held benefits to raise money. A total of $80,000 was raised. Of that amount, $9,000 came from ticket sales of the play, *These Shining Lives*, a Chicago production about the radium tragedy, which gave performances in the Ottawa Township High School auditorium in December 2010.

The bronze statue of a young woman, holding a rose in one hand and a paintbrush in the other, was dedicated on September 2, 2011.

Ottawa has murals on the outside of several downtown buildings. A mural was painted on the outside of the Central Life Building in 2019. It was dedicated to the progress of women. One panel shows an unidentified Connecticut dial painter and another panel shows Charlotte Purcell of Ottawa. This is the building where Andrew O'Conor had his law office in the 1920s and 1930s.

Leonard Grossman deserves a memorial somewhere in Ottawa, too. He took on the case of these powerless women when no other attorney would, particularly the Ottawa attorneys. He worked long and tirelessly, and he not only took no fee, but he paid the legal expenses from his own pocket. Truth and justice were his goals, not money.

Catherine Donohue also deserves special recognition. This modest woman became a symbol of strength, even as she lay helplessly in bed. She fought the corporate criminals, even as her frail frame weighed about 58 pounds after months of the most agonizing pain possible, all the while keeping a strong faith in God.

Margaret Looney, Marie Rossiter, and every other person who painted radium dials did not die in vain. Their suffering led to advancements in medical research on the effects of radium poisoning and led to better laws for the protection of workers.

There never was an acceptance by the owners of Radium Dial or Luminous Processes—no acceptance, no apology, and no money for the hundreds of women they killed or damaged.

Central Life Building, 628 Columbus Street, Ottawa.

The 3-D mural on the side of the Central Life Building in Ottawa, which included the radium workers, was painted in 2019 by John Pugh.

15

AFTERMATH

As for the former dial painters, not all of them died quick, painful deaths. It depended on how much radium, and later tritium, they ingested. Many lived for decades, but almost all of them suffered from damaged bones, lost teeth, blood disorders, and various cancers.

Pearl Payne worked at Radium Dial for just eight months, in 1923 and 1924. She was a very close friend of Catherine Donohue, and she was named as one of the "living dead" in 1938. Pearl lived to the age of ninety-eight, dying in 1998. It is possible, as Pearl wrote, that the radium poisoning went to her organs instead of her bones, and the poison was removed with the tumors. She wrote the following in 1938:

> I believe I was fortunate in the fact that the radium did not become localized in some of the bones of the body, which cannot be removed as is the case with many of the girls that are dead and still alive … Although I am alive after five years of hemorrhages, operations and near-death experiences, I am left with a weak heart and the necessity of taking daily by artificial means the substance which was manufactured by the destroyed organs which were removed.

Pearl Payne had radioactive tumors when she was pregnant, yet her daughter, Pearl Zigler, lived to the age of eighty-nine, dying in 2018.

Two others in the "Society of the Living Dead" from 1938 lived long lives. Charlotte Purcell, who had an arm amputated due to radium poisoning—and who the newspapers named in 1938 as the number two victim (after Catherine Donohue) who would soon die—lived until 1988, dying at age eighty-two.

Marie Rossiter died in 1993 at the age of eighty-seven. Olive Witt died on August 9, 1981 at the age of seventy-nine. Olive had worked at Radium Dial less than a year. Frances O'Connell, another of the 1930s "doomed women," died in 1977 at the age of seventy-one.

The company claimed it told its workers to stop "lip pointing" in 1925. However, some women still did it in order to maintain quick work. Nancy O'Mara told me that her mother, Anne E. Brunick, worked at Luminous Processes during World War II, in addition to sewing parachutes at the Libbey-Owens-Ford plant. Nancy said:

She talked about being instructed to "point her paintbrush" with her tongue ... She also talked about co-workers using the paint on their fingernails. She said their dates would pick them up after work and show off their luminous paintwork. Mom knew that her two war-time jobs were more lucrative than her pre-war jobs had been. She also believed that such work was patriotic. Like most young women of that time, my mom was buying household items for her "hope chest" and felt that the timing of her wartime earnings was fortuitous because she was dating my dad and they planned to get married as soon as the war ended.

When mom recalled her job at Luminous Processes, she remembered feeling wary about the safety of the luminous paint. Despite the welcome wages and sense of patriotism, she expressed being glad she had not worked there any longer than she did.

Anne died in 2007 of lymphoma at the age of eighty-seven. Other women died young, although it took a little longer. Norma (Payne) DeGroot died in 1953, at the age of forty-eight. She was the sister-in-law of Pearl Payne.

Ruth (Ashbee) Williams and her husband Cecil owned Clover Farm Store grocery at 1429 W. Main Street. Ruth died in 1954 at the age of forty-eight. She had worked at Luminous Processes for twenty years, from 1924 to 1944. She weighed 55 pounds when she died from radium poisoning.

When Beatrice Workman died on August 25, 1959, at the age of fifty-four, her husband Thomas told the newspaper that she had suffered from radium poisoning for thirty years. She worked in the Ottawa plant in the 1920s and her complaints were dismissed by doctors. A bone marrow sample showed radium was present. A coroner's jury ruled she died of bone cancer caused by radium.

The "Radium Girls" display in the LaSalle County Museum in Utica.

Helen, Bernice, Georgia, Catherine, and Julia Florence Browne, about 1913. Catherine and Bernice worked at Radium Dial. Catherine died of radium poisoning.

While Catherine (Browne) Reavy died of radium poisoning at the age of thirty-nine, her sister, Bernice (Browne) Callahan (who also worked at Radium Dial), lived to age seventy-one, dying in 1980. Bernice lived at 322 E. Superior Street, two blocks from Catherine Donohue. As an aside, Bernice Callahan and Catherine Reavy were the great-aunts of my wife.

The coroner listed radium as the cause of the cancer that killed Dolores Smith of Ottawa, who died in 1961 at the age of fifty-five. She and her husband, Edward, a maintenance worker at Libbey-Owens-Ford, lived at 723 State Street.

Inez (Corcoran) Vallat died on February 25, 1936. Her husband, Vincent, died on the exact same day in 1985, forty-nine years later, at the age of eighty-one.

Frances and Marguerite Glacinski were sisters who worked at Radium Dial. Frances was sixteen years old when she started work in 1922. Marguerite was sixteen when she started in 1924. Frances married John O'Donnell and they had three children. Frances died in 1977 at the age of seventy. Marguerite died in 1981.

Lottie Murray, the first plant superintendent of Radium Dial in Ottawa, the woman who taught the workers to point the tip of the brushes with their tongues, was another victim of her own deadly business. She died of cancer in Ottawa on July 10, 1927, at the age of forty-nine. She is buried in Mount Olivet Catholic Cemetery in Chicago.

Rufus G. Fordyce, vice president of Radium Dial, died in 1964. He lived until the age of seventy-nine; however, he never directly handled radium.

Rufus Reed died on June 6, 1960, in New Rochelle, New York, at the age of seventy-seven. He was born in Wilmington, New York, in 1883. His draft registration card in 1918 showed he was a cost clerk at Standard Sanitary Manufacturing in Chicago, and that he was deaf. Mr. Reed was assistant superintendent at Radium Dial in Ottawa from 1923, becoming superintendent after Lottie Murray died. After Radium Dial closed in 1936, he became manager of Luna Radium in Westchester County, New York. Mr. Reed was fired from his job a few years later. He was working at Rex Products Company in New Rochelle in 1942, a company that made women's compacts and buttons for military uniforms. By 1947, Rufus Reed was working as a maintenance man at the YMCA in New Rochelle, a job he held for several years.

Not much is found about Mercedes Margaret (McCabe) Reed. She was listed as Rufus' surviving wife in his 1960 obituary. One report says she died in 1971 at the age of eighty-six. This causes me to speculate whether she really ate radium paint off a spatula in the 1920s, as some workers testified. Both Mercedes and her husband knew the dangers at that time, when women in Westbury, Orange, and Ottawa were dying of radium poisoning. Perhaps she ate something else to fool the women. It is doubtful she lived into the 1960s if she had done that. The Reeds lived at 1019 Post Street in Ottawa, just two blocks away from the Browne and Reavy house at 1219 Post Street.

Andrew O'Conor III, the Ottawa lawyer who fought the claims of the Radium Dial women, died in 1942 at the age of sixty-two. His wife, Mary, died in 1940. Their son, Andrew IV, also became a lawyer in Ottawa, and he represented local farmers who fought to prevent additional land being taken for the LaSalle nuclear power plant in the 1980s; he died in 1998 at the age of seventy-nine. They are buried in St. Vincent's Cemetery, LaSalle.

Catherine Donohue's husband, Thomas, died in 1957. He never remarried, and neither of their children had children of their own. Catherine was loaded with radium when she was pregnant with her children. Thomas, Jr., died in 1963, at the age of thirty, of kidney failure caused by Hodgkin's disease. He had worked at Owens-Illinois glass factory in Streator. Mary Jane died in 1990, at the age of fifty-five, after a lifetime of health problems and constant pain.

Mary Jane weight just 10 pounds when she was a year old. Mary Jane grew to about 4 feet and 3 inches. She became a nurse but could not work in a hospital because of her physical limitations. She became a private duty nurse at a nursing home which previously had been the company hospital for Radium Dial. When Mary Jane died, the funeral home was packed with friends and former dial painters.

Marie Rossiter and her brothers, Hank and Bill.

Leonard Grossman died in 1956 at the age of sixty-five. Arthur Magid died in 1970 at the age of sixty-eight.

It was not until 2018 that the identity of the men who tagged the side of the building with "Dial Luminous For Death" was publicly revealed. It was Bob and Michael Barron, from the local environmental group. Michael also was a financial advisor with Edward Jones investments. He died of cancer in 2018 at the age of sixty-five.

The last of the Radium Dial workers lived past one hundred years of age, because their exposure was not as great. Mae (O'Donnell) Keane died on March 1, 2014 at the age of 107. She was born on May 28, 1906 and was eighteen years old when she went to work in the Waterbury, Connecticut, plant in 1924. She did not like the taste of the paint and quit after a short time. Even so, all her teeth fell out by her late thirties, and she also fought colon and breast cancer. Mabel Williams died on July 23, 2015, at the age of 104. She was born on September 8, 1910. She worked in the Ottawa plant for three years but refused to tip the brush to her mouth. Her husband, Elmer, noticed her hair sometimes glowed in the dark. Mabel and her husband are buried in Oakwood Memorial Cemetery in Ottawa.

It brings a scary thought. What if something new came around, and the authorities—doctors, scientists, and government officials—all said it not harmful and actually was good for you? People would happily use it until it was learned it was deadly. By then, it would be too late. It happens all the time with new miracle drugs. One TV commercial heralds a new drug, followed by another commercial from a lawyer willing to sue on your behalf if you took that drug. One day, a study says coffee is good for you; the next day, a study shows it will kill you. One study says the radiation from cell phones is minimal; another study says it may cause cancer. "Scientific facts" change from day to day, as seen in the 1929 *Popular Science* story, and as seen in today's debate on the climate.

Today, people come from all over the world to see the memorial to the "Radium Girls" in Ottawa. The tragedy will never be forgotten. However, rather than something of which to be ashamed and denied, it now is a lesson from which to learn.

Mae Keane.

Mabel Williams.

Appendix

THE WORKERS

Here is a list of employees at Radium Dial and Luminous Processes, which I obtained from the National Archives and Records Administration in Chicago. The names are from the lists of workers studied by Argonne National Laboratory, plus other names they were able to identify as workers, with additional information from the Ottawa and LaSalle-Peru city directories. There are no listings for a number of years in the 1930s, and no names after 1970. This is by no means a complete list. Not every worker was studied by Argonne. The list from the Archives includes the names of the workers, their spouse, their address, the name of the householder, and in some cases, their phone number. Not all workers were dial painters. I include just the names of the workers here. I did not repeat names of people who worked in more than one decade.

The Peru studio, 1922–1923: Irene Arnold, Alma Block, Olga Block, Mary Boyle, Lena Cheise, Elizabeth DeGroot, Emma Delaney, Romilda Delaney, Vivian DeSteiger, Pauline Derwitz, Marie Dwornik, Leona Eickhoff, Bella Ellis, Ruth Faber, Sadie Farrar, Lyda Fitzgerald, Agnes Flynn, Josephine Gende, Mary Gribben, Nicholas Hammer, Della Harbison, Francis Kumacar, Anna Kuzma, Gertrude Lawniczak, Ruth Leyes, Adelaide Liebhart, Katherine Meisenbach, Louise Merz, Inez Montagnoli, Mary Montagnoli, Ruth Morgan, Freida Mosbach, Lottie Murray, Anna Noel, Lavina Noel, Elizabeth Ohligschlager, Catherine Payne, Norma Payne, Mercedes Reed, Rufus Reed, Veronica Sausen, Marie Scholle, William Thompson, Evelyn Tissen, Dora Walter, and Ida Weber.

Radium Dial, Ottawa, 1920s: Mary Anselme, Ruth Ashbee, Alice Bach, Anne Bakalar, Mildred Baker, Alta Ball, Harriet Barnhart, Maxine Becker, Edna Becker, Dorothy Beguin, Elmer Berge, Mildred Bowers, Edith Brandherm, Catherine Browne, Isabelle Bruck, Marie Bruckner, Elsie Brye, Anna Burkhardt, Emma Busch, Nita Capitani, Anna Mae Carpenter, Emma Carroll, Grayce Carter, Reva Carter, Alice Christie, Mary Churchill, Jane Clayton, Ruth Conroy, Inez Corcoran, Alicia Corrigan, Ella Cruse, Berlindes Cusic, Martha Dana, Lulu Defenbaugh, Romilda Delaney, Lenora Dirkes, Edna Daugherity, Marie Divornick, Emily Duchala, Irene Dunham, Mary Duffy, Pauline Durkee, Sadie Dwornik, Mildred Dwyer, Irene Elias, Mary Ellington, Emma Engel, Mabel Engle, Ethel Fargo, Sadie Farrar, Alice Farrell, Lyda Fitzgerald, Mildred Fitzgerald, Veronica

Fitzgerald, Hazel Fornero, Bessie Gallup, Eliza Gardner, Marion Geiger, Frances Glacinski, Marguerite Glacinski, Dalton Goetschius, Joseph Goetschius, Lucille Goldsmith, Sybil Goldsmith, Clarence Grandadam, Christine Halm, Irene Halm, Lucille Hampson, Georgia Hanlon, Ollie Hardy, Anna Harris, Edna Hemmerle, Ruth Herman, Alberta Hetrick, Augusta Hettel, Ella Holm, Nellie Jacobs Houltram, Alice Jehly, Helen Jehly, Leola Kellogg, Mildred Kennedy, Edith Kieber, Mae Kinkie, Agnes Kirwan, Ruth Knox, Margaret Koenig, Florence Komenski, Maxine Kopp, Mary Kusnerik, Marie Laatz, Bertha Lanter, Ethel Larsen, Bernadette Londergan, Margaret Looney, Loretta Lowman, Elizabeth Mann, Edith Marshall, Ruth Mathes, Vera McClusky, Delores McCullough, Mena McKinley, Catherine McLarnon, Madeline Meany, Katherine Meisenbach, Louise Merz, Nell Mickelson, Dorothy Mills, Eloise Moore, Helen Munch, Eileen Munn, Helen Murphy, Lottie Murray, John Naber, Mildred Nelson, Anna Nink, Emma Odenwalder, Dorothy Over, Marion Palmer, Peggy Palmer, Verna Parsons, Mary Paulik, Catherine Payne, Norma Payne, Katherine Peppler, Frances Pollack, Sophia Prafcke, Ula Price, Mamie Rashid, Catherine Browne Reavy, Mercedes Reed, Rufus Reed, Vilda Roser, Marie Becker Rossiter, Izetta Kennedy Saager, Kathryn Sabatha, Mary Sagi, Jeannette Sanford, Zilma Schadewaldt, Pearl Schilling, Perene Shaver, Pauline Skolek, Maxine Smith, Mildred Smith, William Sonntag, Irene Tammen, Evelyn Trost, Mary Turner, Verona Utiss, Florence VanNatta, Agnes Vargo, Mary Vasichko, Cleo Veroni, Mary Vicini, Olga Vicini, Ethel Wagner, Adeline Waldron, Marie Webb, Olive West, Anna Westerwelle, Margaret Wescott, Margaret White, Catherine Wolfe, Margaret Wolfe, Merle Zeilman, Ruth Zeilman, and Matte Zieseness.

Radium Dial, Ottawa, 1930s (some names listed in the 1920s are not repeated here): Vivian Behler, Bernice Browne, Dorothy Butterfield, Mary Elias, Helen Eurick, Mildred Fields, Frances Flamm, Harriet Gray, Loretta Hamalle, Frances Hazard, Edna Hemmerle, Anne Lauterback, Lester Lucas, Margaret Malinowski, Mary Markey, Jewell Mason, Alice Peck, Bentina Peppler, Frances Salawa, Bernice Schinz, Lavon Stafford, Hazel Thompson, Florence Thorson, Robert Turner, Margaret Weber, Hama White, and Helen Woodward.

Luminous Processes, 1930s: Vivian Behler, Martha Dana, Alberta Hetrick, Margaret Koenig, Lester Lucas, Catherine McLarnon, Emma Odenwalder, Peggy Palmer, Mary Peppler, Perene Shaver, Frances Pollack, Sophia Prafcke, and Margaret Weber.

Luminous Processes, 1940s: Gilda Battistelli, Alan Benckendorf, Betty Bischoff, Mary Capsel, Lorraine Caputo, Eva Conrad, Mary Corrigan, Patricia Danner, Patricia Dobbs, Celia Fitzgerald, Mildred Gorman, Betty Gretencord, George Irvine, Patricia Kennedy, Lottie Krafcky, Dorothy Lambert, Mayme Loeb, Lester Mettille, Jeanette Neilsen, Rita Nightingale, Mary Olle, Dorothy Pearson, Evelyn Ponzi, Leota Pool, Doris Repka, William Rohe, Shirley Rowlee, , Mildred Thacker, Robert Turner, Mary VanTrigt, and Laura Young.

Luminous Processes, 1950s: Bert Alsvig, Robert Bischoff, Lois Bounds, Patricia Bucknall, Viola Chase, Lee Chiovatero, Dorothy Crane, Beverly Creed, Beverly Cummings, Ann Day, Meredith Ellis, Geraldine Eyerly, Marjorie Eyerly, Pauline Fuller, Dorothy Griffith, Martha Hartshorn, Dorothy Hynds, Alma Jacobson, Lyla Kolb, Margaret Krantz, Ethel Lee, Mary Licato, Marie Lockhart, Shirley Ludwig, Anita Mennie, Darlene Miller, Anne Maccono, Ivis McGrath, Anita Mennie, June Mennie, Dorothy Oppenlander, Leota Otis, Velma Ott, Eleanor Philpott, Helen Rickerd, LaVonne Robnett, Margaret Rossiter, Rita Rudnicky, Rachel Schinz, Pearl Schott, Laura Strobel, Esther Swiger, Hattie Tieber, Alberta Timmons, Cora Varrato, Betty Vercolio, Ruth Williams, Phyllis Young, William Zorn, and Ethel Zsizsik.

Luminous Processes, 1960s: Fred Beyer, Catherine Calkins, Joyce Couch, Jerry Cox, Michael Fuller, Donald Helffrich, LaVonne Johnson, Ruth Manheim, Ray Mattes, Clara McGinnis, Eleanor Meagher, Mabel Pitts, Donna Railton, Jean Somerville, and John Wells.

Luminous Processes, 1970s: Helen Markut, Marjorie Waterworth, and Delores Wicks.

The Archives only go to the year 1970.

15 WALKING GHOSTS JILTED BY JUSTICE

By JOHN MAIN
(TIMES Staff Correspondent)

Ottawa, Ill., July 7.—Fifteen living dead women will appear before the Illinois Industrial commission here on July 25.

It will be the next-to-the-last act of what lawyers say is the biggest and most pitiful miscarriage of justice in the history of Illinois.

The LAST act will be these women's deaths—sure, tortured, horrible—death that bears a close outward resemblance to leprosy or to a terrible cancer—

Death from "radium poisoning."

More than a year ago, The TIMES revealed the story of these women—the doomed women of Ottawa. Nine already are dead. Fifteen are dying, literally by inches.

Two of the victims are now living in Chicago. One is Mrs. Charlotte Purcell, 31, of 6749 S. Halsted st., mother of three children, Donald, 8; Patsy, 6; Jean Ann, 5. The other is Miss Helen Munch, 27, of 3423 N. Avers ave.

Indicative of the terrible ravages of the "radium" disease, Mrs. Purcell has lost one arm, the marrow of the bones

Poisoned by "radium," Mrs. Catherine Donahue sits at home in Ottawa, knowing each day may be her last. Like her, many women have suffered and died from ravages of disease contracted through working in "radium" factories where no devices were provided to protect them from the gnawing radioactive salts.

Building in Ottawa, formerly occupied by Radium Dial Co., where employes contracted "radium poisoning."

literally eaten away by the action of the radioactive salts that have poisoned her system.

Here in Ottawa, another victim, Mrs. Catherine Donahue, 520 E. Superior st., lives in daily fear that some day—so the doctors tell her—she will open her mouth and her jaw, simply, will fall out, eaten away in a similar manner.

OTHER CASES WORSE

Terrible as these cases are, they are mild in comparison with those of some of the women who already have died, or who linger in horrible agony.

The cases of all closely parallel the "radium poisoning" cases in the New Jersey plant of the U. S. Radium Corp. that shocked the nation in 1929.

These Ottawa women, however, were employed by a small, supposedly independent concern—the Radium Dial Co.

The story of the tragic deaths of those that died and of the horrible suffering of those that remain alive, as told in The TIMES in March a year ago, was, perhaps, sufficiently terrible. One might well have supposed then, perhaps, that the cup of misfortune held by these unfortunates was full to running over.

MORE TROUBLES

Yet, in the past year, additional misfortune, The TIMES now learns, has befallen them.

A year ago they were the doomed women of Ottawa. Today they are the forgotten women.

The hearing before the industrial commission this month will be their last stand—their last hope of collecting damages.

And even here, the law will operate against them.

ONLY $10,000 LEFT

The Radium Dial Co. has closed its plant in Ottawa—has "slipped out from under," leaving only a $10,000 bond posted with the industrial commission.

Thus all these doomed women may hope for, even if they win before the industrial commission, is a share for each of them in this $10,000—less than $667 apiece "on the average."

Of course they sued the Radium Dial Co.

A Chicago lawyer, J. S. Cook, 222 N. Wells st., took their cases, virtually on charity. No Ottawa lawyer—or so the victims here say—would touch them. Ottawa bitterly resented—resents to this day—these poor women's charges as giving a "black eye" to the community.

FILES TEST CASE

At any rate, Atty. Cook filed a test case, in the Superior court of Cook county.

And here began the travesty, the almost unbelievable miscarriage of justice, that, now, has added its disappointments to the doomed women's burden.

No man was at fault, no judge, no lawyer, no court. Simply, the law itself—specifically, Illinois' antiquated, insufficient "Occupational Disease Act."

Illinois has a new occupational disease act now, passed only recently, but passed too late so far as these doomed women's cases are concerned.

It was under the old act that Atty. Cook had to sue—and almost immediately he ran into one of those legal technicalities that makes the layman's blood run cold.

The act, you see, provided that if a person wanted to sue an employer for damages because of an occupational disease, the suit must be started within six months.

But "radium poisoning" takes three to five years to develop to a point where even expert diagnosticians can tell for sure what it is!

And so, when Atty. Cook filed his test case, the Radium Dial Co. did not even bother to deny the women's charges that they had contracted this dread disease while in its employ.

'WHAT OF IT?'

In effect, the company's reply was, "Even if it is true, what of it? Your suit has not been brought within the specified time."

At his own expense, Atty. Cook carried the fight all the way to the Illinois Supreme court. His argument was that the doomed women had a "common law" right, and that no statute could take it away from them.

Moreover, he argued, the statute was not meant to apply to such cases as these. It was absurd, he contended, to say suit must be

Home of Living Dead—home of Mrs. Catherine Donahue, 520 E. Superior st., Ottawa.

(Continued on page 15, col. 1)

ABOUT THE AUTHOR

Jim Ridings was born in Joliet, Illinois. He earned a bachelor of science degree in journalism from Southern Illinois University at Carbondale in 1976.

He was a reporter for *The Daily Times* in Ottawa and *The Beacon-News* in Aurora. He won more than a dozen awards for investigative reporting while at both newspapers, from the Associated Press, United Press International, Copley Press, Illinois Press Association, Northern Illinois Newspaper Association, Aurora Lions Club, SDX Society of Professional

Jim Ridings with Steve Sanders (WGN-TV, Channel 9-Chicago). (*Photo by Laura Keller*)

Journalists, and other organizations. Ridings was presented a Studs Terkel Humanities Service Award from the Illinois Humanities Council in 2006.

Ridings has written more than two dozen books of local Illinois history. Five of his books have won awards from the Illinois State Historical Society. Among his books are *Len Small: Governors And Gangsters* (2009), *Small Justice* (2014), *Cardiff: Ghost Town On the Prairie* (2007), *County West: A Sesquicentennial History of Western Kankakee County* (2003), *Chicago To Springfield: Crime and Politics in the 1920s* (2010); *Greetings From Ottawa* (2006); *Greetings From Starved Rock* (2011); *Images Of America: Ottawa* (2011), *Wild Kankakee* (2012), *The Illustrated History of the Cherry Mine Disaster of 1909* (2020).

Jim and Janet Ridings live in Herscher, Illinois, and have two beautiful daughters, Stephanie and Laura.